theatre & Scotland

Trish Reid

First published 2013 by
PALGRAVE MACMILLAN

Palgrave Macmillan in the UK is an imprint of Macmillan
Publishers Limited, registered in England, company number
785998, of Houndmills, Basingstoke, Hampshire RG21 6XS.

Palgrave Macmillan in the US is a division of St Martin's Press LLC,
175 Fifth Avenue, New York, NY 10010.

Palgrave Macmillan is the global academic imprint of the above
companies and has companies and representatives throughout
the world.

Palgrave® and Macmillan® are registered trademarks in the United
States, the United Kingdom, Europe and other countries

ISBN: 978–0–230–29261–1 paperback

This book is printed on paper suitable for recycling and made
from fully managed and sustained forest sources. Logging,
pulping and manufacturing processes are expected to conform to
the environmental regulations of the country of origin.

A catalogue record for this book is available from the British
Library.

A catalog record for this book is available from the Library of
Congress.

10 9 8 7 6 5 4 3 2 1
22 21 20 19 18 17 16 15 14 13

Printed in China

contents

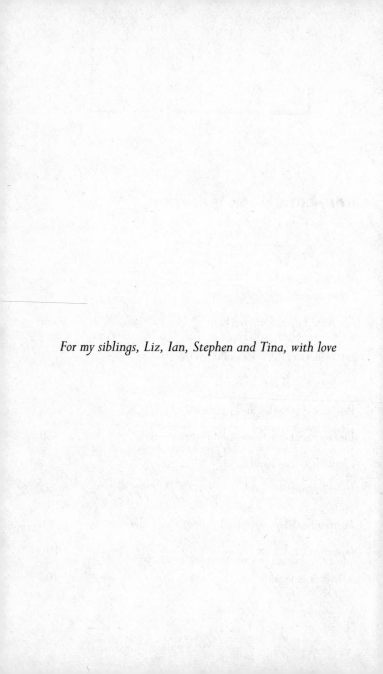

For my siblings, Liz, Ian, Stephen and Tina, with love

series editors' preface

The theatre is everywhere, from entertainment districts to the fringes, from the rituals of government to the ceremony of the courtroom, from the spectacle of the sporting arena to the theatres of war. Across these many forms stretches a theatrical continuum through which cultures both assert and question themselves.

Theatre has been around for thousands of years, and the ways we study it have changed decisively. It's no longer enough to limit our attention to the canon of Western dramatic literature. Theatre has taken its place within a broad spectrum of performance, connecting it with the wider forces of ritual and revolt that thread through so many spheres of human culture. In turn, this has helped make connections across disciplines; over the past fifty years, theatre and performance have been deployed as key metaphors and practices with which to rethink gender, economics, war, language, the fine arts, culture and one's sense of self.

Theatre & is a long series of short books which hopes to capture the restless interdisciplinary energy of theatre and performance. Each book explores connections between theatre and some aspect of the wider world, asking how the theatre might illuminate the world and how the world might illuminate the theatre. Each book is written by a leading theatre scholar and represents the cutting edge of critical thinking in the discipline.

We have been mindful, however, that the philosophical and theoretical complexity of much contemporary academic writing can act as a barrier to a wider readership. A key aim for these books is that they should all be readable in one sitting by anyone with a curiosity about the subject. The books are challenging, pugnacious, visionary sometimes and, above all, clear. We hope you enjoy them.

Jen Harvie and Dan Rebellato

foreword

I'm neither ashamed nor proud to be Scottish. It's simply a matter of fact that I am. I've certainly never wanted, artistically, to be defined in those terms and resent any implication of duty to address my Scottishness dramatically. On the few occasions I have – in my film *The Debt Collector*, for example – the intent has been satirical. I've lived in London for more than twenty years, which is where people go to be generic and die.

So I'm no expert on the current state of Scottish theatre and I can make no claims for Scottish theatre's influence on the larger theatrical culture. Given the annual migration to Edinburgh, I suspect it must have had *some* but I can't quantify it. All I can tell you is the effect Scottish theatre has had on me and how it's shaped my attitude to my profession.

My relationship to Scottish theatre is complex because both my father, Sandy Neilson, and my mother, Beth Robens (her stage name), worked in the industry, as director and actress respectively. I was, quite literally, a rehearsal room baby and have vivid memories of travelling between gigs in 7:84 and Wildcat tour vans whilst various inebriates sang songs about losing people at sea.

It didn't feel glamorous or unusual to me. It fostered a certain pragmatism in that it was our livelihood. The effect of bad reviews or flop shows or 'dry periods' was very real – emotional hurt, loss of money, bailiffs at the door. I had/have no particular love for the business itself. What did fascinate me was the work and particularly its impact on audiences.

Touring was a basic remit in those days – funding depended on it – so shows had to appeal to quite disparate audiences, of varied classes and cultures. Most of the work was political but, crucially, balance was not at a premium. The viewpoint was clear, socialist, and usually hostile towards our oppressors in the South, or their lackeys in Scotland. Whilst this sounds primitive now, it allowed, at least, for passion, for anger, for sheer emotional force. It was designed to inflame.

What was interesting, though, was the sleight of hand employed. This was hot-blooded political theatre with one foot in the music hall. As grim as the subjects often were, much comedy was employed and that comedy was as often 'low' as it was 'high' and parochial in a way that defiantly resisted notions of universality or longevity. Songs and musicianship were frequently central. Even the acting style was heightened; one might go so far as to call it 'muggy'.

Despite my misgivings about the parts, the sum was clearly greater. This broad, accessible style had evolved, not from Brecht or any theatrical precedent, but from a communitarian tradition of storytelling. (I note here that the closest parallel I've encountered was the work of a Nigerian theatre company, which struck me as interesting.)

So when I began my career I had a template for theatre. It should be accessible, it should inspire feeling and it should employ any and all performance skills in doing so. The audiences I wanted to access were younger, the feelings I wanted to inspire were stronger, the techniques I wanted to use were more modern, but otherwise, the apple had not fallen far from the tree.

True or not, my perception, on moving to London, was of a foreign theatrical landscape. There were straight dramas, there were comedies and there were musicals. You saw one or the other. A lot of people who went to one would never, on principle, go to the other. The audiences were overwhelmingly middle-class. There were companies who were trying to cross-fertilise performance skills but they were all labelled as 'experimental'. Realism was the order of the day. Theatre seemed to be doing little that you couldn't get from TV.

I was also aware that – for the overwhelming majority of my generation – theatre was an irrelevance, a rarefied pursuit for the old, the posh, the academic. Seeing what was on offer in this most central theatrical hub, the reasons seemed clear.

I wasn't the only one thinking this way. Simultaneously, several other writers – most famously, Sarah Kane – were formulating ways to break the stasis. This was the beginning of the 'in-yer-face' movement, though that's a somewhat reductive term. For my part, all the taboo-busting that went on was an attempt, however crude, to break down the entrenched detachment of audiences, to disable cerebral defences and force them to *engage*. It was not a consciously rebellious impulse. I was doing what came naturally.

Thankfully, the theatrical landscape of 2012 is a much more colourful place. Companies that would once have been dismissed as 'experimental' are now regular visitors to the West End and the South Bank. New shows tackle serious subjects but employ a rainbow of techniques to do so – comedy and song, of course, but also dance and puppetry and new technologies. In Scotland, the hugely successful *Black Watch* falls easily into the lineage begun in the 1970s and has found global success.

But theatre is not out of the woods. We're losing venues, we're losing funding and we're failing to convince new generations – whose love of interactivity should make them an easy sell – that theatre is worth their time. There's no future in blaming them. We, the practitioners, must look to ourselves. We must constantly re-assess and rejuvenate our training, our methods, our product. Vitally, we must never forget what it is that we are here to do: to reflect, to challenge, but foremost to entertain.

Anyway, that's what I learned in Scotland, in the 1970s, in a tour van, with drunk people singing about losing folks at sea. This book brought it all back.

Anthony Neilson is an award-winning playwright and director. His early plays Normal *(1991),* Penetrator *(1993) and*

The Censor *(1997)* *were closely associated with the 'in-yer-face' movement. More recently,* The Wonderful World of Dissocia *(2004),* Realism *(2006) and* Relocated *(2008) have been widely praised for their formal innovation and daring. In 2010 he wrote and directed the family show* Get Santa *for the Royal Court Theatre. Neilson is among the most imaginative and provocative Scottish theatre artists of his generation.*

theatre & Scotland

Introduction: histories and myths

Why write a book about Scottish theatre? Is there enough that is distinctive about Scotland's performance culture to make a book about it worthwhile? Would it not be more productive and illuminating to examine broader trends in theatre across a wider geographical area? As we are constantly reminded, we live in an increasingly 'global' world in which borders seem ever more porous, cultures more homogeneous and international conglomerates more powerful than nation-states. On the other hand, as the sociologist David McCrone suggests in *Understanding Scotland* (2001), studying the reactions of small nations to broad social and economic pressures often enables us to see the effects of these phenomena more clearly. It might even be argued that patterns of response and resistance are easier to discern in the smaller scale, as McCrone suggests, just as 'the turn of the tide' is more easily monitored by 'observing small boats rather than large ships' (p. 1).

Like a number of commentators, in making this analogy, McCrone posits an understanding of the local and the global – however much tension there may be between them – as two sides of the same coin. Indeed, as Dan Rebellato observes in his 2006 article 'Playwriting and Globalisation', 'the assertion of the local as a site of resistance to the global' has become a recurring motif in the anti-globalisation movement, and it has impacted theatre studies in discussions of the efficacy of site-specific work, for example (p. 98). Debates about globalisation and its effects, such as those staged by Naomi Klein in *No Logo* (2000), have brought the local into focus. Consequently, there has been growing interest in how small nations and territories such as Scotland, Wales, Norway, Catalonia, Québec and the Basque Country respond to global pressures and make their way in an era in which the authority of nation-states seems considerably less secure than it did a century ago. The question of how Scotland, in particular, should best perform itself has become additionally live and pertinent in the aftermath of devolution in 1999, and has been further enlivened by the recent voting behaviour of the Scottish electorate, behaviour that has made a referendum on Scottish independence before 2015 a certainty. Few commentators would confidently predict the outcome of this referendum, or the precise arrangement of the constitutional settlement ten years from now.

One specific aim of this book is to provide a concise overview of the shifting role(s) of theatre and theatricality in contemporary Scottish culture in the context of wider debates about the theatre of small nations in the age of globalisation and devolution. Scotland has a peculiar political, religious and constitutional history that has affected the development of its performance culture in a number of significant ways. Part of the work of this introductory section is to sketch out key areas of historical context and debate in order to provide a basic framework in which to place the discussion of Scottish theatre that follows. A further and related aim of this section, and this book, is to raise the curtain on a theatrical Scotland richer, more varied, raunchier and less uptight than has hitherto been readily imagined. This is a timely endeavour because the idea of Scotland's theatrical inheritance as threadbare and impoverished, and of the Scots as an anti-theatrical people, retains a surprising amount of currency. Most commentators agree, for instance, that the mid-twentieth century witnessed a discernible and sustained increase in theatrical activity in Scotland. However, writing towards the end of the 1970s, Christopher Small, in his foreword to David Hutchison's *The Modern Scottish Theatre* (1977), acknowledges that many still wonder 'whether there is enough of a Scottish theatre to make a study of it' (p. v). More recently, Ian Brown, in his introduction to *The Edinburgh Companion to Scottish Drama* (2011), expresses the hope that the volume will go 'some small way to helping cure the amnesia that has afflicted knowledge about, recognition of and pleasure in Scottish drama and theatre' (p. 5). My hope is that the present book will contribute to the cure.

Like many dominant narratives, the tale of the anti-theatrical Scots is seductively simple. It goes something like this. During the medieval period Scotland boasted a rich tradition of folk and religious drama commensurate with that of any other European nation. Regrettably, in the sixteenth century the Calvinist Reformation crushed this tradition and henceforth the theatre was suppressed in Scotland, principally through the agency of the Kirk (the established Church of Scotland). The reformers were killjoys who banned Christmas and dancing. They were suspicious of pleasure in all its forms, and their specifically anti-theatrical bias stunted the growth of professional theatre in Scotland. It is their zealotry, and their zealotry alone, that explains the absence of a visible and continuous Scottish playwriting tradition comparable to those of Scotland's European neighbours, and consequently of a dramatist equal in standing to Shakespeare, Molière or Calderón de la Barca.

Unsurprisingly, the Calvinist fervour of the reformers is a matter of regret and even embarrassment for many contemporary Scottish commentators. Tom Devine summarised prevailing attitudes to the Reformation in an article commemorating its 450th anniversary for *The Times*:

> In the secular Scotland of this new millennium, the Reformation usually has a bad press. The Calvinist tradition that has moulded the nation is seen through a negative lens. Its malignant influence is said to have spawned intolerance, oppressive social disciplines, an aggressive and

rapacious capitalism, sexual guilt and dysfunc-
tion, and warped attitudes to music, painting and
the creative arts, which have only been changing
in recent generations. ('Thank Calvin for Great
Scots Minds', 10 August 2009)

Devine is in the process of arguing here that the Reformation
– especially in its forceful privileging of literacy for all –
contributed to the growth of Scottish intellectual culture in a
profound and lasting manner. It was an essential precursor to
the Scottish Enlightenment, many of whose leading figures,
such as Adam Ferguson, William Robertson and Thomas
Reid, were themselves ministers of the Kirk or sons of the
manse (that is, their fathers were Church of Scotland ministers). Calvinism, Devine reminds us, was a fiercely cerebral
form of Protestantism. In the aftermath of the Reformation
theological issues were widely debated in Scotland, in lengthy
sermons, in learned pamphlets and in open discussion. This
tradition fed into and supported a fantastic flowering of
Scottish intellectual culture during the eighteenth century.

The notion that the Reformation effectively eradicated
Scotland's performance culture has also been challenged
and complicated in recent work by scholars such as Ian
Brown, Sarah Carpenter, Bill Findlay and John McGavin.
Contemporary Scotland boasts a rich, lively, eclectic and
distinctive performance culture. It seems unlikely that this
culture appeared fully formed in the mid-twentieth century
without drawing on pre-existing performance practices
and traditions, however marginalised and obscured these

traditions had become. Equally, it is absurd to imagine that a group of religious zealots, however committed, could successfully suppress the theatrical impulse of an entire nation for several centuries. Better rather, following Brown, Carpenter, Findlay and McGavin, to consider the ways in which the theatrical impulse was displaced and transformed in Scotland under the pressure exerted by the reformers. This is part of the work of the second section of this book, which considers the importance of folk, amateur and popular drama to the Scottish tradition in the centuries following the Reformation.

As the brief account above illustrates, the history of theatre in Scotland is contested. 'History', it should be noted, has had a problematic and exaggerated significance in Scottish culture. A quick glance, as McCrone observes, 'at the "Scottish" shelves in any major bookshop reveals that much of Scotland seems to be "over", for they are weighed down with accounts of the country's past' (*Understanding Scotland*, p. 129). For centuries key figures and events in the nation's past have been circulated, distorted, sentimentalised and mythologised, in a process of representational overload that has, according to some critics, effectively replaced meaningful focus on the present. Among other things, this demented fixation on figures such as Mary Queen of Scots and Bonnie Prince Charlie contributed to a profound pessimism among Scottish intellectuals, from Hugh MacDiarmid to Tom Nairn, so that, while commentators may vary considerably in method and emphasis, a consensus of sorts exists about the roots of the Scots' predilection for highly selective and sentimentalised accounts of their own history. Since the Treaty of Union in 1707, this argument goes, Scotland has lacked real political agency and has turned instead to over-inscribed historical narratives for a sense of cultural identity. Moreover, Scottish culture has become distorted and stunted in the process.

The most influential and powerful expression of this line of thinking is Tom Nairn's *The Break-up of Britain* (1977): 'The oddity of the Union has always posed grave cultural and psychological problems in Scotland – problems recognisable ... through a characteristic series of sub-national deformities, or neuroses' (p. 118). Nairn is especially scathing about popular and sentimental discourses of 'Scottishness', particularly 'kailyard' and 'tartanry', which he famously describes as the 'vast tartan monster' (p. 162). The kailyard (literally 'cabbage patch') school of Scottish fiction emerged in the late nineteenth century, but the term is currently used to describe any sentimentalised and sanitised representation of Scottish life – particularly rural life – and might include television favourites such as *Dr Findlay's Casebook* and *Monarch of the Glen*. The important thing is that these fictions offer a version of national life at some remove from the harsh realities of urban Scotland. For Nairn, tartanry and kailyard evidence a destructive false consciousness, a neurotic and infantilised national psyche, which he finds frustrating and very disappointing. The thing about the tartan monster, in Nairn's conception, is that it devours everything around it. Continually producing fantasy versions of Scotland and Scottishness, it leaves little room for realist or progressive representations of the nation. Colin McArthur develops this argument robustly in his collection on cinema, *Scotch Reels* (1982), in which he describes the 'seriously stunting effects Tartanry and Kailyard have had on the emergence of alternative discourses more adequate to the task of dealing with the reality of Scottish life' (p. 3).

With the benefit of hindsight, and perhaps especially from a post-devolutionary perspective, Nairn's arguments about the paralysing effects of kailyard and tartanry on Scotland's political progress appear overly pessimistic. In addition, the idea that other discourses in Scottish culture have been entirely squeezed out seems overstated, as the discussion of Scottish theatre that follows will demonstrate. Finally, despite the insights he undoubtedly offers, the tone of superiority Nairn adopts in relation to popular culture is problematic and rather unpleasant. Drawing on the work of the French Marxist philosopher Louis Althusser – particularly his influential essay 'Ideology and Ideological State Apparatuses' (1970) – Nairn conceives of Scottish popular culture as a type of state apparatus that, far from reflecting popular grievance, is employed to control the thought processes of the masses. In this book I am working from a markedly less rigid critical position. I am seeking to show that popular forms have been crucial, integral and beneficial to the development of Scotland's distinctive performance culture. Consequently, the arguments I present in the following sections rely on the assumption that the relationship between the popular arts and progressive politics is fluid and dynamic, and that popular and commercial forms can sometimes be politically engaged and anti-authoritarian.

For several hundred years Scotland's stages have been important sites for engagement with the issues outlined above. The country's past has been represented and misrepresented in numerous productions, reflecting the nation's wider preoccupation with its own history. Barbara Bell, in her chapter 'The National Drama and the Nineteenth Century' (2011), describes in some detail the emergence and subsequent hegemony in Scottish theatre of a group of plays substantially based on the novels of Sir Walter Scott, especially *Rob Roy* (1817), which drew on Scottish history and myth for their subject matter. In the mid-twentieth century a group of dramatists including Robert McLellan, Alexander Reid and Sydney Goodsir Smith produced historical plays inspired both by McLellan's own *Jamie the Saxt* (Curtain Theatre, Glasgow, 1937) and Sir David Lyndsay's medieval classic *Ane Satyre of the Thrie Estaitis* (1554). These plays were part of a conscious effort to rehabilitate the Scots language and to fill a gap created by the perceived absence of a theatrical tradition in Scotland, but they were written in rather contrived forms of semi-archaic Scots, placing them at some remove from the realities of contemporary Scottish life. Since the 1970s, however, fewer Scottish history plays can be located so easily within traditions of kailyard or tartanry. In a chapter titled 'Plugged into History' (1996), Ian Brown demonstrates that among 'the great achievements of the Scottish stage has been the variety and complexity of the ways in which it has dealt with history and the particular significance of this use of the past for the present stage of Scottish culture and history' (p. 85). History plays such as Stewart Conn's *The Burning* (Royal Lyceum, Edinburgh, 1971), Hector MacMillan's *The Rising* (Dundee Rep., 1973) and Donald Campbell's *The Jesuit* (Traverse, Edinburgh, 1976) utilised historical material with the express aim of holding up a mirror to contemporary Scotland.

The most influential and emblematic Scottish history play of the late twentieth century, however – and I want to mention this because its influence has been explicitly acknowledged on more than one occasion by members of the contemporary Scottish theatre-making community, especially the creative team at the National Theatre of Scotland (NTS) – was undoubtedly John McGrath and 7:84 (Scotland)'s *The Cheviot, the Stag and the Black, Black Oil* (1973). McGrath's company was to become one of the most significant in the history of British alternative theatre, and *The Cheviot* its most famous production. In it, as elsewhere in his work, historical material was presented in a dynamic dialectic with contemporary events, so that history was used primarily to shine a light on the present, and in particular to emphasise the extent to which current attitudes represent a falling away from ideological clarity and rigour.

By the early 1970s the discovery of oil in the North Sea had precipitated a boom in new industry in the Scottish Highlands. Always politically engaged and motivated, McGrath recognised that this phenomenon could be seen as part of a larger cycle of exploitation of the area that included the Clearances and the imposition of large sporting estates, as well as the various strictures imposed in the aftermath of the final defeat of the Jacobite armies at Culloden in 1746. *The Cheviot* is formally complex and innovative. In it McGrath utilised the oral performance traditions of the céilidh, which he enriched with tropes such as the double-act and the satirical sketch drawn from popular commercial forms. He also borrowed elements from the armoury of agit-prop, including a portable pop-up set designed by John Byrne, the inclusion of factual information delivered in direct address and representations of real historical figures. All of this was organised in short scenes, with actors playing multiple roles. For instance, as well as playing the MC, and the swindling negotiators Loch and Texas Jim, Bill Paterson created the memorable role of Andy McChukemup, the Glaswegian entrepreneur whose mission is to take full advantage of the influx of 'oil' dollars into the Highlands:

> So – picture it if yous will, right there at the top
> of the glen, beautiful vista, the Crammem Inn,
> High Rise Motorcroft – all finished in, natural,
> washable, plastic granitette. Right next door the
> 'Frying Scotsman' All Night Chiperama – with a
> wee ethnic bit, Fingal's Caff – serving seaweed-
> suppers-in-the-basket, and draught Drambuie.
> (p. 48)

Like all other company members, Paterson was required to play a range of roles, and instruments, showcasing his considerable skills as a comic performer as well as requiring him to address the audience directly in a more serious mode. Key aspects of the production's impact in this respect relied on the careful handling of transitions of tone from satirical swipe to straightforwardly sincere political assertion:

Enter SNP EMPLOYER.

SNP EMPLOYER. Not at all, no no, quit the Bolshevik haverings. Many of us captains of Scottish industry are joining the Nationalist Party. We have the best interests of the Scottish people at heart. And with interest running at 16 per cent, who can blame us?

MC2: Nationalism is not enough. The enemy of the Scottish people is Scottish capital, as much as the foreign exploiter.

Drum roll. (p. 66)

There is a certain irony, of course, in McGrath employing nationalist rhetoric – the 'Scottish people' – precisely in the moment of dismissing nationalism as a political solution, but the thrust of *The Cheviot* nonetheless works consistently to expose as contingent, not inevitable, the economic and political forces that have decimated the Highlands across successive generations, and therefore the play is best understood as an example of materialist theatre practice.

One effect of McGrath's self-consciously jolly dramatisation of Scottish history, as Drew Milne observes in his article 'Cheerful History: The Political Theatre of John McGrath' (2002), is that comedy 'intervenes in the tendency to lament and mourn the past that is constitutive of a backward looking nationalist sentiment' (p. 319). In the event, *The Cheviot*'s influence on a generation of alternative theatre makers cannot really be overstated. As Baz Kershaw observes in *The Politics of Performance* (1992), it 'crystallised a form of cultural production that became increasingly important in the 1970s' (p. 167). Politics aside – if that is ever possible – the production also became important as a stylistic influence, embodying as it did a kind of pronounced folk populism that came to be seen as emblematic of a distinctively Scottish theatre tradition. Its influence can be seen, for example, in the formal organisation, if not the ideological content, of the NTS's internationally acclaimed production of Gregory Burke's *Black Watch* (2006).

Without doubt the most significant development in the theatrical landscape of twenty-first-century Scotland has been the establishment of a national company intended both to articulate Scotland's rich performance traditions and to ensure the continuing development of a confident, dynamic and outward-facing modern Scottish theatre. I have written elsewhere and in some detail – in a article titled 'From Scenes Like These Old Scotia's Grandeur Springs' (2007) – about the long campaign for the establishment of the NTS, but the point I want to make here is that the Scottish performance culture from and into which the NTS was born, and with which it has engaged since 2006, already encompassed a wide range of practices. In addition to the established practitioners and companies, a generation of significant new playwrights such as David Greig, Zinnie Harris, David Harrower, Douglas Maxwell, Rona Munro and Anthony Neilson had emerged and were engaging with issues of Scottish identity directly and obliquely in a range of contexts. Alongside the populist political inheritance of the 1970s, the linguistic strategies employed by Scottish playwrights in the 1980s – including Liz Lochhead, Iain Heggie and Chris Hannan – were an important source of inspiration for these writers. In an interview with Mark Fisher for Anja Muller and Clare Wallace's volume of essays on his work, *Cosmotopia: Transnational Identities in David Greig's Theatre* (2011), David Greig explains:

> These writers show you can write in your own poetic ideolect, which is very connected to real language and dialect, but is actually your own synthetic creation. No one in the world speaks like a Chris Hannan character, but his language is nonetheless obviously founded in east Glasgow. (p. 17)

For Greig this earlier generation of Scottish playwrights had established the foundations on which he and his fellow writers of the 1990s could build their work:

> theatrically, the sense of what a Scottish playwright ought to be, that landscape had been made for us by all the writers of the 1980s ... we don't have to do any of that work, we don't have to prove our 'Scottishness'. (p. 18)

Clearly, Greig sees himself as part of an evolving tradition. By the time the new NTS began producing work in 2006,

Scotland boasted a number of innovative theatre companies, such as Greig's own Suspect Culture, Grid Iron, Vanishing Point, Poorboy and Theatre Cryptic, which produced work that was often site-specific and strikingly contemporary. This wide range of work was, and has been, brought into dynamic relationship with the new company.

The NTS began well. Its constitution as a buildingless company was widely acclaimed and has since been borrowed by the national Theatre of Wales. The appointment of Vicky Featherstone, formerly of Paines Plough, as its first artistic director was also well received. Moreover, the critical success of its inaugural season, which included the *Home* project, Gregory Burke's now legendary *Black Watch* and Anthony Neilson's *Realism* (Royal Lyceum), was profound enough to provoke something akin to nostalgia among newspaper critics in their reviews of the decade in late 2009. For Joyce MacMillan, writing in *The Scotsman* on 17 December 2009, the NTS 'emerged as an iconic 21st century institution, born of the times we live in' (p. 17). In the event the company's – and especially *Black Watch*'s – impact was as unpredicted as it was stunning. The newly established NTS may have had international success in its sights, but it can hardly have expected to achieve this in the first year of operation. Opening at the Drill Hall, Forest Hill, Edinburgh, on the night of 5 August 2006, *Black Watch* quickly became the must-see production of that summer, going on to win numerous awards, including four Oliviers and a New York Drama Critics' Circle award for Best Foreign Play, and to tour extensively at home and abroad. Revivals of the production have toured abroad in almost every year since its première, and it has become emblematic both of renewed confidence among Scottish theatre makers and of a distinctively Scottish approach to the medium.

In his director's note to the published text (2007), John Tiffany explicitly locates his production in the tradition epitomised by *The Cheviot*:

> Fuelled by variety, visual art, music and a deep love of storytelling, Scotland's artists have created a form of theatre that is as significant and vital as its written drama. It features narration, song, movement, stand-up comedy, film, politics, and above all an urgent need to connect with its audience. (p. xi)

However, as well as drawing consciously on these traditions, the production also bore traces of its own historical moment. Sections based on the transcripts of interviews conducted by Gregory Burke with members of the famous Scottish regiment, for example, drew on verbatim practices, while the movement direction by Frantic Assembly's Steven Hoggett owed more to the developing traditions of physical theatre than to those of variety and music hall. Nevertheless, Tiffany cites McGrath's play as an 'inspiration behind the ambition of *Black Watch*' (p. xii).

Although it is not my intention to offer a lengthy critique of *Black Watch* in this introductory section, it is worth noting that while the production shared a number of stylistic features with *The Cheviot*, it mobilised 'history' to very different ends. Put simply, McGrath sought to challenge establishment versions of history and replace them with a people's history that would reveal the mechanisms through which workers had been oppressed, in order that these mechanisms might be challenged. In *Black Watch*, Burke constructs a narrative of working-class male solidarity achieved through regional and generational commitment to military service within the context of the British Empire. Importantly, this martial tradition is figured as essentially and authentically Scottish, and the machismo inherent in its practice is neither fully interrogated nor problematised. On the contrary, Burke conjures Scotland's mythic past in support of the notion of this martial tradition as authentically Scottish, insisting in his introduction to the text that when 'the clans of Scotland used to fight they would have people who stood in front of the soldiers and recited the names of their ancestors' (p. xiii). Worryingly, the extent to which Scotland's highland regiments were implicated in the imperial project and its attendant crimes is never properly acknowledged. In *The Cheviot*, by contrast, one character describes his relationship with the Native Americans as follows: 'They give me furs, beaver skins, Davy Crockett hats and all the little necessities of life. I give them beads, baubles, VD, diphtheria, cholera, fire water and all the benefits of civilization' (p. 73).

Despite, or perhaps even because of its chauvinism, the success of *Black Watch* evidences the continuing efficacy of theatre in contemporary Scotland. In 2007, the newly elected SNP government mounted two gala productions to mark the opening of the parliamentary session. *Black Watch* seemed so marvellously Scottish. Its production values, its confident use of a range of media, the skill of its performers, its topicality, all seemed to reflect and even embody the country's new-found cultural confidence. Moreover, as well as offering a soldier's-eye view of the second Gulf War, *Black Watch* mobilised key elements of the internationally recognised iconography of Scotland: the tartan, the bagpipes, the kilt and the Scottish soldier. In the next section of this book I want to examine this iconography more carefully and consider how it has been utilised in the performance of Scottishness in a variety of contexts. I will argue that while such performances are not always explicitly theatrical, they are always performative in the sense that they constitute expressive actions that intervene in the course of history and events.

Performing Scottishness

Typically, the construction of national identities relies on the circulation of narratives – part truth, part legend – that invest nations and nationalist projects with coherence and intent. Scotland, as we have already established, is a country famously prone to dwelling on and mythologising its own past. For this reason, the dominant myths that constitute Scottishness are worth summarising here, because it is partly through engaging with them that Scotland's theatre makers have contributed to, and problematised, debates about national identity and the 'imagined' shape of a new Scotland in a time of increased political and institutional agency. Historically, and somewhat problematically, as McCrone notes, 'those identities diagnosed as arche-typally Scottish' have been almost exclusively masculine (p. 142). Women, when not excluded entirely, have been relegated to supporting and domestic roles. The iconic image of socialist industrial Scotland, or Clydesideism, for example, was a skilled male worker. The myth of the 'lad o' pairts', or the clever young Scot able to rise from humble origins thanks to an open education system, included no analogous 'lass o' pairts'. Discourses of 'tartanry' largely circulate around the Scottish soldier, and the martial tradition he embodies. Thankfully, the dominance of these masculinist constructions of the nation has been challenged in recent decades, not least by contemporary theatre practitioners who have both given voice to marginalised sections of the community and highlighted the distance of real men from dominant notions of hegemonic masculinity. This work will be considered in more detail in the final section of this book; in the present section my aim is to reflect on one discourse of archetypal Scottishness and its utilisation in the performance of national identity at home and abroad.

Scotland is a country – and perhaps it is unique in this – whose performance of identity utilises a distinctive woven cloth. This cloth, tartan, has been an important element in the performance of Scottishness for several centuries and its efficacy as a signifier is apparent in many contexts, not least the establishment by the US Senate in 1998 of National Tartan Day, an annual holiday designated in celebration of Scottish Americans. Tartan, its history, its appropriation by and association with various constituencies, its commercialisation and proliferation, its widespread adoption as a contemporary national costume – especially in the form of the short kilt or philibeg – offers a useful prism through which to view shifting conceptions of Scottish identity and its performance.

As the discussion of kailyard and tartanry in the previous section suggests, the term 'tartanry' was, for much of the twentieth century, typically used pejoratively to describe the vulgar commercialisation of tartan and its employment in reductive, stereotypical, and often comic, performances of Scottishness. Particular ire was reserved in this discourse for Scotch music hall and variety acts, among which Sir Harry Lauder's (1870–1950) was the most celebrated. According to Cairns Craig, in his essay 'Myths against History: Tartanry and Kailyard in 19th-Century Scottish Literature' (1982), the 'turning of the back on the actuality of Scottish life is emblematically conveyed in the figure of Harry Lauder – Kailyard consciousness in tartan exterior – who evacuates from his stage persona, indeed from his whole identity, the world of the Lanarkshire miners from which he began' (p. 13). For Craig, at least in this essay, the extravagant incongruity of Lauder's stage persona – combining exaggerated Highland dress and sentimentalised Lowland speech – makes a mockery of Scottish history and culture. Lauder has betrayed his industrial roots – a sin for which there is presumably no forgiveness. The celebrated modernist poet and nationalist Hugh MacDiarmid was similarly vociferous in his condemnation. Writing in the *The Stewartry Observer* on 23 August 1928, he insisted:

> 'Lauderism' is, of course, only the extreme form of those qualities of canniness, pawkiness and religiosity, which have been foisted upon the Scottish people by insidious English propaganda, as a means of destroying Scottish national pride, and of robbing Scots of their true attributes which are the opposite of these mentioned. ('Scottish People and Scotch Comedians', p. 5)

Given MacDiarmid's high-minded project it is perhaps not surprising that he found the absolute ease with which Lauder's jaunty, humorous and sentimental constructions of Scottishness attracted English applause troubling. His assertion that tartan comics were somehow a product of English propaganda is without evidential base, however. As Paul Maloney shows in a recent essay, 'Ethnic Representation in Popular Theatre' (2010), Lauder's act was by no means without precedent in Scotland; it was in fact a development of indigenous practice and specifically a product of Scotland's expanding urban entertainment culture (p. 134). Doubtless Lauder's utilisation of tartan was intended as a joke, but jokes can be complex and subtle, and their effects various and contradictory.

Underwriting the many insults hurled at Lauder is an unwillingness, or perhaps inability, to appreciate the subtlety of popular performance modes and the complexity of the cultural transactions they encoded, not to mention the obvious pleasures audiences derived from them. The most reductive accounts of Lauder's act, such as those quoted above, imply his performances lacked nuance, irony or tonal range. The influential English critic James Agate, in *Immoment Toys* (1945), thought otherwise:

> It must not be supposed that Lauder does not calculate his effects. He does. Each verse is more elaborate than the preceding one, so that the effect is both cumulative and culminative … Soldier, sailor, yokel, god's innocent are all to their several manners born. They are true to nature, yet transfigured … The gist of it is not the superimposing of absurdity upon plain sense, but the discovery of the rational in lunatic or sentimental disguise. When all is said and done the man remains an evangelist whose tidings are of pure joy. (pp. 201–2)

Agate was the drama critic for *The Sunday Times* from 1923 to 1947, and his vivid account undoubtedly brings us closer to a full understanding of Lauder's charismatic appeal. If Lauder's success locally and nationally was significant, his impact overseas among Scottish settler communities, and especially in the United States, was spectacular. Beginning in 1907 he made more than twenty visits to America, and also toured extensively in Australia, Canada and the Far East. These activities demonstrate both an acute sensitivity to national and international markets and the widespread appeal of tartanry for audiences at home and abroad.

The derision with which many high-minded twentieth-century Scottish intellectuals – perhaps especially intellectuals of nationalist persuasion – greeted Lauder's performances, and others like them, also stemmed from the conviction that tartan was an ancient and traditional cloth which should be treated with a degree of reverence. Its importance as a cultural signifier, in their view, was derived from its historical associations, specifically with the Highlands and the Gàidhealtachd, and consequently with resistance, rebellion and the pre-industrial past. It is, we might note, this cluster of associations on which Mel Gibson drew when costuming his William Wallace in tartan plaid for the multi-Oscar-winning film *Braveheart* (1995). In fact, as a Lowlander who conducted much of his campaign from a forest near Selkirk in the Borders, Wallace would never have worn Highland dress, nor would he have painted his face blue or gazed at the glory of Glen Nevis from a craggy adjacent peak. Gibson, however, had little interest in historical accuracy, preferring to draw shamelessly on iconography linking tartan and the Highlands explicitly with rebellion and resistance. This link was in fact forged in the aftermath of the Jacobite rebellions of 1715 and 1745, four centuries after Wallace was executed in 1305. It is at this point that tartan becomes not only the national but the rebel cloth.

The final defeat of the Jacobite armies at Culloden in 1746 was followed by harsh reprisals on the part of the

Hanoverian government. Highlanders were stripped of their right to bear arms and the *Act of Proscription* (1746) placed severe restrictions on the wearing of tartan:

> Any persons within Scotland, whether man or boy (excepting officers and soldiers in his majesty's service), who should wear the plaid, phili-beg, trews, shoulder belts, or any part of the Highland garb, or should use for great coats, tartans, or parti-coloured plaid, or stuffs, should, without the alternative of a fine, be imprisoned for the first conviction for six months, without bail, and on the second conviction be transported for seven years. (ch. 39, s. 17)

As well as confirming tartan's status as the rebel cloth, paradoxically, these restrictions had the effect of concretising the image of the Scottish soldier as kilt and tartan wearing, and of the kilt itself as a kind of costume. For several decades the British army became the only legitimate forum in which tartan could be worn. The Highland regiments consequently exploited to the full, on the parade ground and on the battlefield, tartan's peculiar efficacy as a marker of sartorial exhibitionism, as a textile of excess. At the same time, as Jonathan Faiers notes in his book-length study *Tartan* (2008), significant numbers of Scottish nobility defied the new law by continuing to wear tartan, if only in private and in specially commissioned portraits. From this period, the wearing of tartan became 'a vestimentary demonstration of Scottish nationalism' and political allegiance and not necessarily of clan or local association (p. 42). Thus, by the end of the eighteenth century tartan had already acquired a fluid identity. Depending on context it could draw on associations with the Highlands, with familial and regional loyalties, with discourses of rebellion and resistance, with Scottish nationalism, with the project of Empire via the regiments and with the extravagant and aggressive performance of Scottish masculinity.

If this were not enough, tartan was further popularised in the nineteenth century via its association with British royalty. The pageantry of George IV's visit to Edinburgh in 1822, for which the monarch wore full Highland dress, complete with pink tights, was followed by Queen Victoria's acquisition of Balmoral in 1852. These events initiated a craze for all things Scottish among the British aristocracy. As well as spending several months of the year in the Highlands, Victoria and her consort, Prince Albert, performed their shared Stuart ancestry – however distant it was in reality – by furnishing the house in various flavours of Stuart, or the anglicised 'Stewart', tartan and by hosting and attending a range of Scottish entertainments and activities. The royal family's association with the Braemar Highland Gathering continues to this day, for instance. In this way, as Murray Pittock shows in his essay 'Plaiding the Invention of Scotland' (2010), the 'ideological reinscription of tartan on a discourse of British loyalty was achieved' (p. 44). That is not to say that the 'difference' tartan encoded was entirely effaced. As Pittock also notes, by making 'Jacobite-related images and tableaux central to her Scotland', Victoria was able to assert her affinity with 'primitive peoples (like the Jacobite Highlanders) who had suffered defeat throughout her empire', while the success of the Scottish regiments abroad served as a pristine example of how 'picturesque peoples from all over the world might be incorporated' into the imperial project (p. 44). To some extent Balmoralism and the various classificatory systems that surrounded it served to domesticate tartan, but its disruptive and exotic potential never quite disappeared.

For one thing, as the example of Lauder shows, despite the best efforts of cultural and political elites tartan never quite lost its association with exhibitionism and subversion, and it is these qualities that have been most fully and consistently exploited by commercial entertainers since the late nineteenth century. For example, like Lauder, the Glasgow comic Tommy Lorne (1890–1935) often wore a kilt. Unlike Lauder, however, Lorne eschewed the traditions of kailyard and instead drew on European and Victorian clown traditions, appearing in white makeup and white gloves. His long, expressive hands and lanky figure were combined with a shortened and somewhat feminised version of the kilt and accompanied by a droll delivery. For Paul Maloney:

> [in] reframing Highland dress in jauntily absurd-
> ist vein, Lorne was not dismissing tartan or
> what it represented: he was rather ironically
> reclaiming it for urban working-class audiences
> for whom its romanticised rural associations

> meant little. Lorne's gentle satirizing of the kilt
> provides a corrective, by resituating tartan and
> the kilt as one part – but not the defining fea-
> ture – of a modern Scottish identity. ('Ethnic
> Representation in Popular Theatre', p. 141)

Lorne was of Irish extraction and his breakthrough performances were in the annual pantomime at the Royal
Princess's Theatre, later the Citizens, in the Gorbals area of
the city, at that time home to a large Jewish as well as Irish
immigrant population. While it would be foolish to imply
that Lorne's appropriation of tartan in the 1920s and 1930s
constituted a straightforward or unproblematic expansion
of the cloth's narrow ethnic and regional associations, his
work nevertheless signals the possibility of such inclusive-
ness. At the Scottish Parliament in 2011 the recently elected
Nationalist MSP Humza Yousaf swore his oath of allegiance
in Urdu, wearing a traditional Pakistani suit supplemented
with a tartan sash, and the popular Scottish folk musician
Andy Chung appears to have little difficulty reconciling his
Chinese heritage with the wearing of a kilt. A more provocative example of hybridity was provided by the reli-
ably controversial Glaswegian comedian Jerry Sadowitz,
who appeared at the Leicester Square Theatre in January
2011 – payot curls dangling from underneath his top hat
– wearing a kilt with a tiny sheep for a sporran and a false
beard. Sadowitz introduced himself as the Scottish Jewish
poet Rabbi Burns. Jokes such as this are broadly amusing but
they also present images of Scottish identity that connect

the present with the immigrant past, just as Humza Yousaf's sartorial choice does. In Scotland, the kilt is now the chosen garment for formal occasions such as graduations and weddings for most men, even in the Lowlands and Borders, although neither is historically a kilt-wearing region.

Aesthetically, the essence of tartan is in its patterning. Within a rigid grid of vertical and horizontal lines, potentially endless colour combinations are possible. It is a cloth at once instantly recognisable but also infinitely variable and playful. Over several centuries and for a variety of reasons it has become synonymous with a number of virtues believed to be characteristically and authentically Scottish, including martial valour and masculine exhibitionism. As Faiers notes: 'The evidence gathered from early paintings and other sources of multiple tartan-wearing, expresses a freedom that predates the nineteenth century's pathological desire to document classify and divide' (p. 48). Arguably this freedom is best expressed currently in the performance practices of the Tartan Army, the colourful band of self-appointed ambassadors who follow the exploits of Scotland's national football team. Foot soldiers of the Tartan Army have increasingly sported the kilt on overseas missions since the 1980s, but they have done so in combination with Timberland or biker boots, outsized tam-o'-shanters decorated with pheasant feathers, glengarries, Native American headdresses and Viking helmets. Here the tartans on display tend to be generic, Black Watch or Royal Stewart, signifying a unified Scottishness but no particular clan or regional allegiance.

It is tempting, as Faiers acknowledges, to read this parodic display as a 'subversion of 'the Highland regiments' (the original tartan army) tartan colonizations', especially since these football fans are famed for their friendliness and good humour, even in defeat (p. 128). The Tartan Army is also usefully considered as a site for the nostalgic performance of working-class male identity, which can be played out boldly, good-naturedly and safely in the carnival atmosphere surrounding each game. In a chapter titled 'Class Warriors or Generous Men in Skirts?' (2010), Hugh O'Donnell surveys accounts of the Tartan Army in the foreign press that repeatedly evidence the good will afforded the supporters throughout continental Europe, and he notes that reports invariably stress 'the good nature and friendly behaviour of the fans' (p. 222). O'Donnell also notes that the European and world football authorities have appropriated the Tartan Army – 'or more exactly the tartan Army discourse' – as an object of desire, showering it with fair-play awards and commendations (p. 228). Considered in this light the Tartan Army appears a considerably less subversive force, especially when one considers that as a unified and unifying construction, it also functions to efface the deeply unpleasant sectarian divisions that continue to define Scottish football at the domestic level.

Such is its flexibility, then, that tartan's meanings can range from the conservative to the radical depending on the context in which it is employed. A relatively conservative use of the cloth, for instance, is a feature of the numerous heritage events staged by the large Scottish diaspora overseas, especially in the United States, Canada, Australia and New Zealand. In this context tartan is used almost exclusively to signify Scottish ancestry and thus to assert a distinctive ethnic identity, the right to wear it being explicitly related to bloodline. The Caledonian and St Andrew's Societies established by early immigrants to offer support to new settlers invariably instituted these events in celebration of their culture. Long before 6 April – the anniversary of the Declaration of Arbroath 1320 – was officially designated National Tartan Day by the US Senate in 1998, large Highland games and gatherings had been a feature of Scottish American life. If nothing else, their scale evidences the importance of the public performance of Scottishness among the diaspora. In Scotland itself the largest is the annual Cowal Highland Gathering at Dunoon, which attracts between fifteen and twenty thousand visitors. The Grandfather Mountain Highland Games in North Carolina, by comparison, has an annual attendance of fifty thousand people.

While Tartan Day events are largely conservative in flavour, the successful utilisation of tartan by the punk fashion designer Vivienne Westwood in the 1970s evidences its continuing efficacy as a rebel cloth, as does its use in the work of Jean Paul Gaultier, John Galliano and especially the late Alexander McQueen. McQueen's fifth collection, the controversially titled 'Highland Rape' (winter 1995–96), featured a catwalk covered in bracken and heather and used distressed models clothed in slashed and revealing garments. Many of the outfits used McQueen tartan bodices, or breast-exposing jackets, trimmed in tartan grafted onto synthetic fabrics and finished with distressed lace. McQueen was, as was to become obvious, consciously recalling the darker side of Highland history. As Caroline Evans observes in *Fashion at the Edge: Spectacle, Modernity and Deathliness* (2003):

> Whereas Westwood's tartans evoked swaggering eighteenth-century individuality, Alexander McQueen's 'Highland rape' collection reprised a harsher moment, the eighteenth-century Jacobite rebellion and the nineteenth-century Highland clearances that McQueen referred to as genocide. (p. 26)

McQueen's collection referenced both the fragility of the Highland way of life and the barbarity of its detractors and victimisers. 'Highland Rape' epitomised the use of tartan as a subversive, problematising and performative medium but it also represented a return to history and as such provides a useful link into the next section of this book.

Practices: popular and political

As noted in the opening section of this book, the National Theatre of Scotland's *Black Watch* earned widespread acclaim for, among other things, embodying and reinvigorating Scotland's eclectic and populist theatre tradition. John Tiffany's production utilised a mixture of song, dance, invective and comedy and employed a range of linguistic registers, while privileging the vernacular. This kind of politicised populism had become a signature of Scottish theatre in the twentieth century through the work of Glasgow Unity in the years after the Second World War, and subsequently through the agency of 7:84 (Scotland) and its musical offshoot Wildcat. If, as Tiffany asserts, the harnessing of popular forms for serious ends is a hallmark of Scottish theatre, then the origins and trajectory of this practice are worth tracing. My aim in this section, therefore, is both to document the resilience of popular forms in the face of historical pressures that were peculiar to Scotland and to suggest that these pressures shaped the Scottish theatrical tradition in positive as well as negative ways.

Before the Reformation, which occurred in the mid-sixteenth century, there was no public theatre in Scotland and playgoing did not exist as a commercial leisure activity. This was in no way an exceptional state of affairs, of course, since it more or less describes the situation across Catholic Europe throughout the period. Importantly, it does not mean Scotland lacked a rich performance culture. As well as court revels, royal processions, minstrelsy, folk plays, dances and guising, Scots took part in the public rituals and ceremonials associated with various Catholic feast days, including Candlemas and Corpus Christi. Such events invariably involved lavish processions sponsored by the burghs and trade guilds, as they did elsewhere. In her chapter 'Scottish Drama until 1650' (2011), Sarah Carpenter provides a detailed and lively account of these practices, and of the range of ways in which they interpolated subjects into the Catholic world-view. Importantly, these events harnessed the power of the burghs themselves, and of the trade guilds, in the consolidation of the interplay between spiritual and secular identities that constituted medieval Scottishness. As Carpenter observes:

> Even as processions these grand events give us some sense of the religious significance of performance and its important role in devotion. The records suggest a powerful mixture of magnificence, pageantry, the emotive and the awe-inspiring. The 'credil & thre barnis [babies] maid of clath' (Dundee, mid-fifteenth century) or the tormentors and cord drawers at the martyrdom of St Erasmus (Perth, 1518) imply vivid and emotional sensation; the 'gold fulye [foyle] to Cristis pascione' and 'makyn of dragone' for St George (Lanark, 1507) suggest spectacular splendour; while the banners, torches and musicians all draw participants and onlookers into a passionate public enactment and celebration of their faith. (p. 8)

Carpenter is drawing heavily for evidence here on what remains the most authoritative and detailed study of medieval performance in Scotland, Anna J. Mill's *Mediaeval Plays in Scotland* (1924). Mill recorded performances of various and contrasting kinds, including royal entries staged by the burghs to welcome monarchs and their spouses and widespread popular practices such as sword dancing and the appointment by town councils of various manifestations of the Lord of Misrule – for example, the Abbot of Unreason, the Lord of Bonacord, and Robin Hood and Little John – to oversee seasonal festivities. However, although Mill was a prodigious scholar, a very real difficulty in accurately documenting Scottish performance traditions in this period stems from the absence of continuous records such as court accords, council registers or the accounts of craft guilds. There is nothing in Scotland to compare, for example, with the English Church Warden's Accounts, from which so much key information about medieval drama in England has been gleaned. Consequently, although it might seem reasonable to assume they occurred across the country, the only burghs that we know for certain supported religious plays similar to those performed in the great English cycles of York and Chester were Edinburgh, Perth and Aberdeen. No plays survive. Scotland formally broke with the Roman Catholic Church in 1560, and while the reformers may not have been as absolutely and uniformly anti-theatrical as has previously been believed, they did actively suppress the feast days with which a number of communal performance traditions had been closely associated, especially Corpus Christi, which was essentially a celebration of the doctrine of transubstantiation, which they abhorred.

Sadly, very few Scottish play texts survive from the period before 1650. The significance of the Latin tragedies of George Buchanan (1506–1582) will be touched on in the next section of this book; otherwise, by far the most extensively reviewed and celebrated is Sir David Lyndsay's (*c*.1490–*c*.1555) satirical morality play *Ane Satyre of the Thrie Estaitis*. Importantly, it is in Lyndsay's masterwork that we first encounter the combining of popular forms with political intention that John McGrath and John Tiffany were to draw upon more than four hundred years later. First performed in the mid-sixteenth century, *Thrie Estaitis* was revived, in a version edited by Robert Kemp and directed by Tyrone Guthrie, to widespread acclaim in 1948 at the second Edinburgh International Festival, and again in the 1980s by the Scottish Theatre Company under the direction of Tom Fleming. With characteristic prescience, John McGrath created an updated version for the Edinburgh International Festival in 1996, adding a fourth estate, the 'Meeja' (media), and the arch-villain Lord Merde, an Australian international media tycoon.

In its original form the *Thrie Estaitis* is an extraordinarily linguistically rich play in which a variety of registers are employed skilfully. Dating from the period before the Union of the Crowns in 1603, it is written in Scots, which remained the language of the Scottish court until after the death of Elizabeth I and the move of the Stuart court south. In foregrounding the expressive possibilities of Scots, the Guthrie revival in 1948 became an important inspiration for a resurgence of Scots-language writing for the stage and shone a light on the complex and often fraught relationship between English and the other main language groups north of the border. In terms of a distinctively Scottish theatrical tradition, the play is also of interest because of the way in which it shifts freely between performance styles and genres, combining elements of farce, biting satire, didacticism and high-moral seriousness. Sir David Lyndsay was the son of a nobleman from Fife and spent his career at the court of the Stuart king James V, where, serving variously as usher, court poet and European envoy, he eventually rose to the position of Lyon King of Arms, Scotland's principal herald. Consequently, his extensive knowledge of the political situation at home and abroad left him well placed to be chronicler of the times. The *Thrie Estaitis* is a lengthy, and confident, play, and as Sarah Carpenter notes, its sophistication evidences both 'an experienced author and a developed tradition' (p. 17). There is surviving evidence of two outdoor performances of the play, one at Cupar in Fife in 1552, and another on the Greenside playfield in Edinburgh in 1554 in the presence of the Queen Regent, Mary of Guise, who was James V's widow and the mother of Mary Queen of Scots.

Thrie Estaitis is unusually long by modern standards: the Edinburgh performance is believed to have lasted all day. It is a play in two parts. The opening section tells of the well-intentioned but naïve and foolish King Humanitie, who, at the instigation of irresponsible associates, embarks on a passionate affair with Lady Sensuality. This inevitably distracts him from his proper responsibilities, which makes room for the rise of Falsehood, Flattery and Deceit. Disguised as clerics, these Vices deny Good Counsel access to the King, and happily gorge themselves while the kingdom sinks into chaos. Chastity and Verity arrive and are duly consigned to the stocks. Eventually Divine Correction intervenes and the King is instructed to call a Parliament of the Three Estates – Nobility, Clergy and Burgesses – to put the kingdom in order. After an earthy and realistic comic interlude in which a pauper is cheated of his last coin by a corrupt cleric selling pardons and fake relics, the second part of the play shifts from the court to the public sphere of the parliament. In a sequence symbolic of their moral turpitude the Three Estates enter backwards, led by their vices. At this point, Johne the Common-weill, the symbolic representative of the people, steps forward and passionately denounces the Vices and the Three Estates, especially the clergy. The merchants and the nobles are contrite, express their willingness to reform and call for Good Counsel, but after a failed attempt to play for time the clergy are stripped of their vestments and exiled from the kingdom. Johne is robed in fine garments and takes his seat at the heart of the parliament, which then passes a series of reforming decrees. The Vices are hanged or banished, and the play ends with a sermon on folly, which serves to demonstrate that the King is now capable of ensuring the well-being of the kingdom and all of its subjects.

As this short summary demonstrates, the *Thrie Estaitis* is notable for the way in which it engages directly with the political issues of its day – especially the profligacy of the clergy – in the presence of a large and socially diverse audience. It calls directly on the monarchy to take a lead in moral and religious reform. It makes extensive use of costume, spectacle, song and direct address as well as vernacular and formal Scots in its analysis of the moral condition of the state. Lyndsay stops short of engaging directly with doctrinal matters, but the play is clearly animated by a reforming zeal, and openly challenges the authority of the Catholic Church as a custodian of the Christian tradition. It is the earliest example (and remains one of the most vivid) of a distinctive combining of popular forms with political invective that was to become a signature of the Scottish performance tradition.

In describing the rich tapestry of practices that made up Scotland's performance culture during the sixteenth and seventeenth centuries, of which *Thrie Estaitis* was part, Mill points out that much of the surviving evidence for folk drama, guising, dancing and various festivities associated with the turning of the year is actually to be found in post-Reformation church records. Typically what is recorded is the Kirk's involvement in acts of censure against people engaged in popular performances of a type derived from their pagan ancestors. For example, Mill records an incident in which five men were summoned at Aberdeen in 1605 for parading through the town 'maskit and dansing with bellis' at Yule (*Mediaeval Plays in Scotland*, p. 13). She also notes that in January 1623, a group of guisers in Elgin were censured by the kirk session (the local church court) because they 'past in ane sword dance in Paul Dunbar his closs and in the kirkyard' (p. 13). The gravitation of these revellers towards the kirkyard is interesting, since it suggests an appetite for transgression that has not been entirely suppressed by the reformers. As John McGavin has shown in his award-winning study *Theatricality and Narrative in Medieval and Early Modern Scotland* (2007), far from being de-theatricalised, Scottish culture continued to be rich with 'events of a theatrical nature' (p. 2).

Clearly, the leaders of the sixteenth-century Presbyterian Reformation held anti-entertainment convictions, and were suspicious of performance in all its forms. However, they also understood that what McGavin describes as the 'battle over the visual semiotics of public life which became acute in the environment of reform, and particularly of contested reform', was a crucial one (p. 19). The reformers intended to win this battle, of course, and while most commentators acknowledge that they succeeded in stifling the development of what might be called a legitimate or authorised drama in Scotland, there is also strong evidence that the theatrical impulse, far from being suppressed, was either incorporated into the practices of the Kirk itself or displaced into popular forms in which it continued to thrive despite the half-hearted disapproval of the reformers. Margo Todd's study *The Culture of Protestantism in Early Modern Scotland* (2002) utilises an abundance of source material from kirk sessions to provide a detailed and persuasive account of how the Kirk balanced the exercise of control with social service. What emerged was a distinctively Scottish Reformed culture in which traditional ritual and drama, and even Catholic imagery, were not abandoned, but rather re-costumed in Protestant garb. Todd demonstrates, for instance, that the sacrament of penance, far from being discarded by the reformers, 'remained in practice a rite of the kirk' and 'actually expanded to become arguably the central ritual act of protestant worship in Scotland' (p. 129).

> Penance was effectively scripted, with allowances for prescribed, formulaic utterance and *ex tempore* speech, the whole inserted into the larger script of sermon-centered worship … the audience, itself controlled by strict rules of acceptable action [was] expected to perform the proper response to the penitent's dramatic display. (p. 19)

Ian Brown, in his chapter 'Public and Private Performance: 1650–1800' (2011), has also shown that far from being monolithically anti-theatrical the Kirk actively encouraged 'school and university drama both in Latin and English' throughout the eighteenth century, providing it carried an appropriate message (p. 23). In addition, the Kirk was not uniformly intent on suppressing local or seasonal customs, and often either turned a blind eye or encouraged modification of such practices in line with the reformers' message. In short, popular performance traditions persisted. The storytelling aspect of the céilidh, for instance, remained prominent until at least the beginning of the twentieth century, and many Scottish social dances continued to have underlying or even overt dramatic structures. Moreover, a strong tradition of popular song, from political ballad to lament, continued to run deep in Scottish culture.

Partly because of the absence of a continuous distinguished playwriting tradition in Scotland, it is tempting to assert a continuous and coherent tradition in popular forms. The task of evidencing such a popular tradition is extremely difficult, however, not least because older forms tend to mutate and develop in response to changing local conditions and exist largely outside the historical record. Certainly, it is possible to argue, as Paul Maloney has done in *Scotland and the Music Hall, 1850–1914* (2003), that there was some connection between seasonal celebrations in Glasgow and the exponential growth of the music hall in the city. Supporting this argument, Elspeth King, in a chapter titled 'Popular Culture in Glasgow' (1987), describes the rich and varied performance culture that grew up in the nineteenth century around the Glasgow Fair, a traditional labour holiday celebrated in July. Originally a rural fair dating from the Middle Ages, from the 1820s the fair became increasingly urban in character, focusing exclusively on entertainment and attracting 'travelling showmen, circuses and freak shows from all over Britain with a wonderful variety of acts' (p. 157). The peripatetic working practices of many performers at the fair would have ensured Glasgow was connected to popular performance traditions as they developed across Britain during the nineteenth century, and thus that it was well placed to develop a rich and distinctive music hall culture of its own.

From the mid-nineteenth century in urban centres, and especially in Glasgow, music hall became increasingly popular, so that by 1900 it could be accurately described as 'national' in terms of what it represented on the stage and the people it employed and celebrated. In April 1887 weekly attendance at halls in Glasgow was estimated by the city's *Evening News* at 40,000 and, although obviously class-inflected, the *News*'s commentary illuminates the symbiotic relationship that existed between those who organised and delivered the entertainment and their audience:

> The music hall has too great an influence with a large portion of the public to be ignored. The best thing to do then is to recognise it, and to endeavour to elevate the moral tone of its patrons. When the morality of those who frequent the music hall is raised to a higher standard, rest assured the management and artists will follow. It is bread and butter with them to keep pace with their audience. (p. 4)

Subsequently, the music hall influenced the development of a modern form of Scottish pantomime, again directed at predominately popular and working-class audiences. Houses for the pantomime were huge. According to *The Glasgow Harlequin*, during the 1895–96 season attendance at the pantomime in Glasgow was 60,000 a week (p. 1). The pantomime season was regularly extended until Easter. In summary, as well as being profoundly vernacular, Scottish music hall and pantomime featured iconoclastic, interactive styles of performance, incorporating songs, sketches and material specifically reflecting Scottish working-class life and urban experience.

The combined power of these traditions, and particularly the intensity of their relationship with the popular audience, was to influence Scottish theatre making throughout the twentieth century, especially among companies and groups with progressive left-wing agendas. Inspired by the wider Unity Theatre movement, Glasgow Unity Theatre, for example, was established in 1940 and went on to become arguably the most influential company of the mid-century. Bill Findlay, in his introduction to *Scottish People's Theatre: Plays by Glasgow Unity Writers* (2008), provides a concise overview of the work of the company, arguing that the best of its work demonstrates the 'perennial potentials of Scottish theatre' (p. xxi). As well as introducing working-class audiences to international classics such as Maxim Gorki's *The Lower Depths*, Sean O'Casey's *Juno and the Paycock* and Clifford Odet's *Awake and Sing*, Glasgow Unity created a repertoire of new Scottish plays that combined traditions of political theatre and popular entertainment. Among these, by far the most commercially successful was Robert McLeish's *The Gorbals Story* (1946), which ran for more than 600 performances between 1946 and 1949 and remained in the repertoire until the company's untimely demise in 1951. Set in a crowded lodging house in the Gorbals area of the city during the post-war housing crisis, McLeish's play utilised Glasgow's rich demotic speech patterns to full comic effect and by doing so tapped into music hall's

strong association with constructions of communal identity, addressed as it was to a working-class Glaswegian audience. On the play's opening night at the Queen's Theatre a
spokesman for squatter's rights spoke passionately from the
floor to an audience that included the city's Lord Provost
and other dignitaries, an event that recalled the intervention of Johne the Common-weill in Lydsay's *Thrie Estaitis*
almost four centuries earlier.

If *The Gorbals Story* was Unity's great money-spinner,
Ena Lamont Stewart's *Men Should Weep* (1947) became its
recognised classic. Like *The Gorbals Story*, it utilised the
vernacular, local reference and humour in focusing on the
effects of poverty on working-class Glaswegian communities. It did so in a way that established a paradigm of Scottish
theatre. An acclaimed revival of the play by 7:84 (Scotland)
in its landmark Clydebuilt season of 1982 was a major fac-
tor in securing its reputation, and it has recently been given
main-stage productions by the National Theatre in 2010 and
the NTS in autumn 2011. Set in a Glasgow tenement during the depression, Lamont Stewart's play is unusual for its
time in that it focuses primarily on female experience, is
relentlessly critical of male behaviour and offers a damning,
if subtle, critique of assigned gender roles. Its central character, Maggie Morrison, a long-suffering wife and mother,
is weighed down by the daily grind of making ends meet.
Her husband, John, is affectionate but jobless and partial to
a drink. Her troubles multiply. Her youngest son, Bertie, is
hospitalised with tuberculosis. Her eldest, Alex, returns to
the overcrowded tenement with his quarrelsome wife, and

the Morrisons' headstrong daughter Jenny leaves home to set up house with a married man. Maggie also has responsibility for her ailing mother-in-law. As they camp out nightly on their living-room floor, Maggie and John wryly fantasise about improved circumstances:

JOHN Some day we'll hae a real bed, Maggie.
MAGGIE Yin on legs? Aff the flair? I havnae been on yin o' they since I wis in the Materity wi Marina. Right enough, it wis lovely ... (p. 78)

As well as allowing her characters to use humour as an antidote to suffering, Lamont Stewart borrows elements of music hall and variety in her staging of tenement life. Maggie's nosey neighbours, Mrs Wilson and Mrs Harris, owe much to the traditions of the double-act, for instance. Finally, it is worth noting that in the 1947 version *Men Should Weep* has a particularly bleak ending in which Maggie dies in childbirth, John falls off the wagon, Alex murders his unfaithful wife and Bertie dies of tuberculosis. Perhaps because of the significant gains made by the women's movement during the 1960s and 1970s Lamont Stewart revised the text for Giles Havergal's 1982 revival, allowing Maggie to survive and achieve some control over her situation.

As I have already noted, according to most accounts the synergetic coupling of the popular with the political in Scottish theatre reached a high point in the 1970s with *The Cheviot*. Although different in style and appeal, Glasgow Unity's work remained an important inspiration for 7:84

because it evidenced the existence of a workers' theatre tradition in Scotland on which the company could draw. Unity was also important as an example of a collective grassroots working practice. It was formed by the amalgamation of a number of politically committed amateur theatre groups, including the Glasgow Corporation Transport Players, the Glasgow Workers' Theatre Group and the Jewish Institute Players, all of which shared a progressive socialist agenda. It ran an 'Outside Group' that took sketches and short reviews to factory canteens, hospitals and trade union meetings. As well as influencing the practices of other politically committed companies such as 7:84 and its musical offshoot Wildcat in this regard, Glasgow Unity can be credited with developing a model, admittedly on a relatively small scale, that has shaped the practices of the NTS. Of the ninety or so projects staged by the new company between February 2006 and December 2010 only about thirty were conventional main-stage or touring shows for adult audiences. The national company's emphasis has been on new, site-specific work and on education, outreach and community projects.

As John McGrath observes in *A Good Night Out* (1981), 'if a theatre company wants to speak to the working class, it would do well to learn something of its language' (p. 56). The language of the Scottish popular audience does not consist exclusively in the various forms of Scots, English and Gaelic spoken in particular areas; it also includes traditions of popular performance passed down from generation to generation. The extent to which popular modes — vernacular and profane language, local references, the mixing of comedy and pathos, audience interaction, the incorporation of music and song – continue to influence Scottish theatre making into the twenty-first century is evident across a range of practices. Anthony Neilson's critically acclaimed *The Wonderful World of Dissocia* (Theatre Royal, Plymouth, 2004) and *Realism* (NTS, 2006) might be cited as examples, as might David Greig's 'play with songs' *Midsummer* (Traverse, 2008).

More recently, Greig's *The Strange Undoing of Prudencia Hart* (NTS, 2011) reaches back beyond music hall and variety to utilise older popular forms. Drawing, via Walter Scott's *Minstrelsy of the Scottish Border* (1802), on the conventions of medieval border ballads – including their rhyme, meter and supernatural themes – *Prudencia Hart* is performed by a small group of actor-musicians in pubs, howfs and function rooms and not in traditional theatre spaces. It begins:

> It's difficult to know where to start
> With the strange undoing of Prudencia Hart.
> Beginnings – as she herself often says –
> Find characters *in medias res* – (p. 3)

Twenty-eight-year-old Prudencia Hart, folklorist and academic, has devoted her life to the study of border ballads. On a winter's night she travels to Kelso in the Scottish Borders to collect song material for her thesis, 'Paradigms of Emotional Contact in the Performance and Text of Traditional Folk Song in Scotland 1572–1798'. She is caught up in a lock-in with a bunch of locals, where she hears of the existence of a song beyond song, an original and uncollected song, a song of undoing. While hiding in the ladies toilet planning her escape – she is not good at parties – Prudencia spots a card advertising a local B&B at Goodman's field and steps out into the snowy night, dazed and confused. Her subsequent journey takes her into supernatural realms. At the final stroke of midnight Nick, from Goodman's field, appears to lead her to shelter:

> Every book that's ever been is here and every book that's never been as well. There's also a pretty extensive collection of rare vinyl. Explore. Take your time. You have an eternity. (p. 55)

Subsequently, she spends two thousand years with the Devil – for Nick is he – researching in his archive and being drawn in by his strange methods of seduction. They fall in love. She is rescued by a colleague, but in the play's dénouement, in the culminating act of the lock-in session – itself a forum for the performance of traditional and popular forms of entertainment – she finally understands that 'to find your song' you must 'first find who to sing it to' (p. 82). Prudencia belongs with the Devil. 'Ideally', according to Greig, 'the song she sings is Kylie Minogue's "Can't Get You of My Head"' (p. 83).

As the celebratory, or even ecstatic, combining of folk tradition with contemporary popular cultural references that characterises *Prudencia Hart* exemplifies, the persistent re-occurrence of popular motifs and forms – from David Lyndsay's *Thrie Estaitis* to traditional forms such as the céilidh, from fairgrounds and music halls to the workers'

theatre movements of the twentieth century and beyond –
is evidence that a powerful popular impulse continues to
drive Scottish performance culture. This is not to say that
Scotland has failed to engage with more 'serious' or 'aesthetic' forms of theatre – the relationship between high-
and low-cultural forms in this area has been complex and
nuanced – but to note that Scottish culture does differ from
that of other parts of the UK in a number of significant
ways. The practice of this difference, whether conscious or
unconscious, goes back at least as far as the Reformation,
the union of the Scottish and English crowns in 1603 and
the union of parliaments that followed in 1707. Since then,
conflicting affiliations to Scottishness and Britishness have
been a subject for constant debate. It may be that the anti-
entertainment prejudices of the reformers stifled the development of a legitimate theatre culture in Scotland and thus
displaced theatrical energy into popular forms, but it may
also be that the popular has simply been the more effective
mode for exploring and problematising Scotland's unique
historical circumstance and for asserting its difference.
As David Mayer notes in his seminal chapter 'Towards a
Definition of Popular Drama' (1977), popular performance
can be seen as antithetical to aesthetic drama in its tendency
to subordinate aesthetic concerns to 'the exigencies of public rite, whether political, religious or social' (p. 265). The
popular continues to be a vital medium through which the
Scottish nation performs itself to itself. But this is not to
imply that Scotland's performance culture is particularly
parochial or inward looking.

Engagements: national and international

By the 1990s Scotland's engagement with European and international contexts had become a distinctive focus in its theatre. Nadine Holdsworth, in 'Travelling across Borders: Re-Imagining the Nation and Nationalism in Contemporary Scottish Theatre' (2003), explores some of this territory in relation to David Greig's *Europe* (Traverse, 1994) and Stephen Greenhorn's *Passing Places* (Traverse, 1997), arguing that 'these plays challenge inflexible notions of the Scottish nation and Scottish cultural identity by presenting both in constant states of production, which are never complete and subject to the play of history, culture and power' (p. 25). For Holdsworth, such plays insist that Scottish identity be conceptualised as contingent and relational, and therefore by implication they challenge reductive, essentialist and triumphalist conceptions of the nation. Contemporary tensions between essentialist and heterogeneous conceptions of national identity will be explored more fully in the next section. This section prepares the ground for that discussion by considering the range of ways in which Scottish theatre has engaged with discourses of nationalism and internationalism in the recent and more distant past.

David Greig's career as a playwright, along with those of his contemporaries Stephen Greenhorn and David Harrower, was enabled by the reinvigorated Scottish theatre culture they entered in the early 1990s. In particular, as the brief discussion in the introduction to this book demonstrated, a number of Scottish playwrights who had come to prominence in the 1980s – including Liz Lochhead, Iain Heggie and Chris Hannan –were important in establishing the foundations on which writers of the 1990s could build with relative freedom and with an internationalist and European focus. The 1980s had seen other welcome developments in the international dimensions of Scottish theatre. For example, the staging of Peter Brook's *Mahabharata* (1985) at Glasgow's Tramway in 1989 had established the theatre as an international performance venue. It went on to host the first Scottish appearances of international artists such as Robert Lepage and the Wooster Group. In the 1990s experimental companies such as Suspect Culture, Theatre Cryptic, and Boilerhouse benefited from the Tramway's Dark Light Commissions programme, and they were followed in the new millennium by a younger generation of companies that included Vanishing Point, Grid Iron and 12 Stars. The 1980s had also witnessed the development of strong international links by the Traverse in Edinburgh and the Tron in Glasgow, and the establishment of companies with a distinctively international outlook, such as Communicado (1983). Among Communicado's successes, Liz Lochhead's *Mary Queen of Scots Got Her Head Chopped Off* (1987) and Edwin Morgan's acclaimed Glaswegian Scots translation of Edmond Rostand's French classic *Cyrano de Bergerac* (1992) were marked by linguistic inventiveness and the company's signature energetic ensemble work. In their exuberant use of Scots, both productions served as positive examples of how the national linguistic resource could be exploited for theatrical effect.

Morgan, who was to become the country's first 'Makar', or Poet Laureate, in 2004, attracted widespread critical acclaim for his translation of Rostand, but he was by that time working in an established tradition. Translation has been an important aspect of the Scottish stage's engagement with other traditions and cultures since at least the Second World War. Glasgow Unity included translations of Ibsen, Lorca and Lope de Vega and a Scots translation of Gorky's *Lower Depths* by Robert Mitchell in its repertoire, alongside indigenous plays. However, the key text in opening up the possibilities of Scots as a medium for translation was Robert Kemp's joyous prose adaptation of Molière's *L'Ecole des Femmes* as *Let Wives Tak Tent* (Gateway, Edinburgh, 1948). This production inspired a cycle of 'MacMolières', celebrated in Noel Peacock's study *Molière in Scotland* (1993). Notable subsequent translations included Liz Lochhead's *Tartuffe* (Royal Lyceum, 1986) and her rendering of *Le Misanthrope* as *Miseryguts* (Royal Lyceum, 2002). The Scottish love affair with Molière can be partly explained in the context of close and centuries-old cultural and political links between France and Scotland. However, in her introduction to *Miseryguts*, Lochhead offers another explanation by noting how readily the French dramatist submits to the populist mode:

> If there is whiff of a certain vulgarity in the air, a music-hall broadness, surely this is better than the stilted and mannered orthodoxies of the Comédie Française? ... We might go a little bit

light on the philosophy but at least in Scotland
Molière is funny. (p. ix)

The love affair came full circle in 2008 with Lochhead's
own translation into rhyming Scots of *L'Ecole des Femmes* as
Educating Agnes (Theatre Babel, 2008). This is not to suggest, however, that Molière was the only dramatist translated for the Scottish stage in the post-war period.

In his chapter 'Talking in Tongues' (1996), Bill Findlay
surveys the landscape of translation for the Scottish stage
between 1970 and 1995. He notes, by way of example, that
the Traverse premièred fourteen translations of new plays
during the period 1980–1995. Besides Molière, two writers
emerged in this period 'with whom Scottish audiences seem
to a feel a special affinity: The Italian dramatist Dario Fo and
the Quebecer Michel Tremblay' (p. 189). As well as linking
this trend to a new confidence among Scottish theatre makers and a desire to engage in direct conversation with foreign stages, Findlay argues that 'Scottish translators are at an
unusual advantage in the English-speaking world in having
at their disposal such a rich and flexible linguistic resource'
(p. 192). Translators could choose to work in standard
English, in normative or demotic Scots, in Gaelic, or in any
combination thereof. Like Morgan and Lochhead they could
choose to invent their own theatricalised brand of Scots/
English. Such levels of choice can be vexed as well as liberating, however, because language is inextricably linked
in Scotland with ethnicity, social class and the after-effects
of Union. A translator's choice of stage language is never

neutral, but always political, whether implicitly or explicitly. The use of demotic Scots, for instance, can signal an effort on the part of the dramatist to connect with the urban working class, as it did for Robert Mitchell of Glasgow Unity or Alex Norton in his translation of Dario Fo's *Non Si Paga! Non Si Paga!* as *Can't Pay? Won't Pay!* (Theatre About Glasgow, 1987), which directly referenced Scottish popular resistance to the poll tax. On the other hand, John Byrne's version of Gogol's *The Government Inspector* (Almeida, London, 1998) used demotic Scots to symbolise the small-mindedness of provincial nineteenth-century Russian society for a London audience. It should also be noted that the most prolific and admired translator of the post-war period, Robert David MacDonald, worked exclusively in standard English.

During his time working alongside Giles Havergal and Philip Prowse at the Glasgow Citizens (1971–2003), MacDonald produced more than seventy translations from ten different languages. His remains the outstanding contribution to translated drama on the Scottish stage during the second half of the twentieth century. MacDonald's translations gave the theatre's Glasgow audience access to a European repertoire – including works by Brecht, Büchner, Dürrenmatt, Genet, Goethe, Gogol, Goldoni, Ibsen, Pirandello, Racine, Sartre and Schniztler – unrivalled anywhere in the UK. John Corbett summarises MacDonald's achievement in his chapter 'Translated Drama in Scotland' (2011):

> The Citizen's company mined European drama
> as a rich resource for striking camp, romantic

attitudes – many of MacDonald's heroes and heroines … are self-destructive artistic figures suffocated by the conventions of bourgeois society. The plays were often brilliantly designed and directed, and their accessibility was guaranteed by a cheap pricing policy that attracted a loyal student audience as well as locals willing to risk fifty pence on the chance of being provoked, titillated, outraged or bored. (p. 102)

The Citizens company offered Glasgow a glimpse of another world. What Corbett describes as their 'perceived otherness … or at least their perceived Englishness' was complicated by the fact that MacDonald and Havergal were born in Scotland and their self-consciously effete stance was not as out of step with the city's wider culture as theatre commentators imagined. The city's 1970s music scene, for instance, produced Postcard Records, whose flagship band, Orange Juice, performed a version of Glaswegian masculinity that was as radically fey as it was liberating and certainly as anti-machismo as anything produced at the Citizens. Contrasting MacDonald's use of English as the medium for translation with the use of Scots elsewhere need not imply criticism of it, therefore. On the contrary, it is only by considering his achievement alongside those of the numerous other Scottish translators that the richness and diversity of the current tradition can be fully articulated. In the post-devolutionary context we might note that David Greig's adaptation of Euripides' *The Bacchae* (NTS, 2007), which featured Alan Cumming clad in gold lamé kilt in the role of Dionysus, owed more to the high-camp tradition of the Citizens than anything else.

The Bacchae was first performed at the Edinburgh International Festival (EIF), and the NTS has had a consistently high profile at the summer festivals since it began producing work in 2006. Its first season included *Black Watch* on the Fringe and Anthony Neilson's *Realism* as part of the EIF. The relationship between the festivals and the wider Scottish theatre community has historically been more vexed, however, and is worth exploring because the summer festivals represent a window through which Scotland has viewed international performance cultures and vice versa. It is important to bear in mind by way of context that the EIF was joined from its inception in 1947 by the Fringe – although this name was not applied until 1948 – and by the Film Festival. In 1950 the Military Tattoo was established. Other annual festivals continued to emerge in the city, including the Jazz Festival in the late 1970s, the Book Festival in the early 1980s and, most recently, the Art Festival in 2004, making the combined summer festivals the largest arts event in the world.

From many perspectives the festivals have been a remarkable success, not least in terms of attendance figures. Iain Crawford, in *Banquo on Thursdays: The Inside Story of 50 Years of the Edinburgh Festival* (1997), gives an attendance figure of 180,000 for the inaugural festival in 1947 (p. 14). In 2004, the summer festivals recorded a combined attendance of just over 2.5 million. Artists of international standing in music, the visual arts, dance, opera and theatre have consistently featured in the programme for the EIF, which attracts audiences from across the globe. In 2010 box office takings were £2.67 million. These figures are important for a number of reasons, not least that with the decline of heavy industry in the post-war period the festivals have acquired increasing importance to the economy of the city and the country as a whole. The EIF aims, according to its website, both to reflect 'international culture to audiences from Scotland' and to provide 'an international showcase for Scottish culture'.

Despite its undeniable achievements, the EIF has attracted sustained criticism. The consensus has been, as Hutchison puts it in *Modern Scottish Theatre*, that its 'contribution to Scottish theatre has been disappointing' (p. 122). This notion – that the EIF has been less than relevant to the development of an indigenous tradition – is supported by its absence from the index of the recent *Edinburgh Companion to Scottish Drama* (2011). Critics have also repeatedly made the accusation that the EIF represents a bourgeois imposition on the city. In his history of modern Scotland *No Gods and Precious Few Heroes* (1981), Christopher Harvie recalls that 'in the 1960s, to defend it in the Edinburgh City Labour Party was like publicly kicking an old-age pensioner' (p. 138). The final and related complaint is that the EIF is not Scottish enough. This last strand of criticism is as old as the event itself. In a letter to the *Glasgow Herald* in February 1947 Hugh MacDiarmid expressed regret that 'the festival authorities have not seen fit to make adequate representation of Scottish music in their programme'. My aim in this section is not so much to refute these criticisms – which have some truth in them – as to qualify them by locating the EIF within a wider tradition in Scottish internationalism that stretches as far back as the sixteenth century.

Scotland has long been a nation of migrants and travellers. For example, the acclaimed humanist scholar George Buchanan spent much of his early career working in France and also taught in Italy and Portugal. Alongside translations of Euripides from Greek into Latin he composed two significant Latin dramas of his own, *Jephthes* (1554) and *Baptistes* (1577), which were to have significant impact in Germany and, most tellingly, in France. As Bill Findlay notes in *A History of Scottish Theatre* (1998), in Germany Buchanan's 'plays were performed before court society and contributed to the development of Jesuit school drama', while in France they influenced 'the great French classical dramatists of the seventeenth-century golden age in French literature: Corneille, Racine and Molière' (pp. 23–24). The close relationship between Scotland and France that Buchanan's tragedies evidence was supported by the 'Auld Alliance', an arrangement that dated from 1295, when the Scottish king John Balliol and Henry IV of France signed a treaty against Edward I of England. One effect of the alliance – which was really predicated on a shared hostility towards England – was that until the end of the eighteenth century significant numbers of Scots were educated in French universities. The eighteenth century also witnessed the Scottish Enlightenment, an explosion of intellectual activity whose influence was felt in continental Europe and in the American colonies. In the wider context, centuries of migration and the consequent establishment of a large and diverse diaspora underwrote Scotland's internationalist outlook. In the twentieth century internationalism of a different kind flourished in the industrial complex of the Clyde, where left-wing and even revolutionary politics took a firm hold. Thus, the call to working-class solidarity made by companies such as Glasgow Unity and 7:84 (Scotland) can be understood as being as much British and international as Scottish. If the Scotland obsessed with its own past described in earlier sections of this book seems at odds with the one described here, this dynamic tension, between the inward and outward looking, should be understood as a key driver of Scottish cultural discourse. The Edinburgh festivals provide an exemplary site for the exploration of these tensions.

Jen Harvie, in her article 'Cultural Effects of the Edinburgh International Festival' (2003), describes the circumstances in which the EIF was established in the immediate aftermath of the Second World War. In particular, she emphasises the extent to which the Festival made a 'meaningful material contribution to the post-war re-articulation and potential regeneration of European culture' at a time when much of central Europe was in ruins (p. 14). During the war, the great artistic cities of the continent had suffered considerably more physical devastation than the Scottish capital, and although Edinburgh did not emerge unscathed from the six-year conflict, it was well placed to provide the necessary spaces – theatres, concert halls, hotels and restaurants – for an international event of considerable scale. To its credit, Edinburgh City Council demonstrated the will as well as the means to host the event. Among the many positives, it can be noted that, as a multi-arts festival, the EIF has managed to maintain a significant degree of diversity despite being programmed by a single director. As Harvie emphasises, it is 'by offering a programme made up of many arts, from theatre to music, dance, opera and visual art', that the EIF is able remain 'relatively distinctive amongst its peer Festivals' (p. 15).

In the remainder of her article, Harvie complicates many of the criticisms typically levelled at the festivals in Scotland. She notes, for instance, how far the celebrated EIF production of David Lyndsay's *Thrie Estaites* in 1948 – and its revivals in 1949, 1951, 1959, 1973, 1984, 1985 and 1991 – 'testified to the EIF's commitment to Scottish culture' and further observes that 'Scottish drama and theatre have been increasingly well represented as the Festival has continued' (pp. 17–18). This has demonstrably been the case over the past decade, when a significant number of new Scottish plays have been commissioned by the EIF. To David Greig's *The Speculator* (1999) and *San Diego* (2003) can be added Douglas Maxwell's *Variety* (2002), Anthony Neilson's *Realism* (2006), David Harrower's *365* (2008), Rona Munro's *The Last Witch* (2009) and Alistair Beaton's *Caledonia* (2010). In 2005 alone, Harrower's Olivier-winning *Blackbird* was commissioned alongside Shan Khan's *Prayer Room* and Chiew Siah Tei's *Three Thousand Troubled Threads*. In addition, the EIF's undeniable elitism has been counterbalanced since its inception by the Fringe, which operates a democratic, non-selecting policy. The Fringe has also provided a major platform for experimental Scottish companies in recent years. Grid Iron established its reputation with a site-specific production of Douglas Maxwell's breakthrough play *Decky Does a Bronco* (2000), for instance, while Vanishing Point's *Subway*, a futuristic and highly visual piece, won a Fringe First and a Herald Angel in 2007. In light of these developments, the Edinburgh festivals appear considerably more engaged at a national level than they did thirty years ago, while continuing to provide Scottish audiences with access to the work of artists of international standing.

At the national level, questions of how Scotland's performance culture should best present itself at home and abroad became additionally live and pertinent in the aftermath of devolution in 1999 and subsequently with the establishment of the National Theatre of Scotland in 2004. Since its inaugural season in 2006 the NTS has retained central significance, attracting praise for its buildingless model and for bringing the work of Scottish theatre makers to national and international audiences. In an effort to establish its forward- and outward-looking credentials, in February 2006 the new company launched with ten simultaneous site-specific productions: *Home Aberdeen*, *Home Caithness*, *Home Dumfries*, *Home Dundee*, *Home East Lothian*, *Home Edinburgh*, *Home Glasgow*, *Home Inverness*, *Home Shetland* and *Home Stornoway*, each made by an established theatre practitioner in collaboration with local artists. This was a bold move. By virtue of its geographical diversity, pronounced regionalism and eclectic mix of styles, *Home* performed a confidently modern and heterogeneous Scotland, in the process allaying the fears of onlookers anxious to see the new company avoid essentialist or reductive constructions of the nation. As a result of their site-specificity, the *Home* performances were able to evoke local memories in a range of ways not usually associated with mainstream theatre practice or traditional theatre spaces. Several brought the past and the present into dynamic conversation. Matthew Lenton's *Home Caithness*, for example, was staged in a disused glass factory, and Wils Wilson's *Home Shetland* on board the North Link ferry that connects the islands to the mainland. Both sites brought into play specific non-theatrical material histories of their own.

Since its inception the NTS has attempted to strike a balance between small-scale events that satisfy the appetites of Scotland's diverse communities across all age groups and larger main-stage productions capable of advertising Scotland's theatre culture to national and international audiences. Overall, the company has continued to favour small-scale projects, but the early success of *Black Watch* – which despite its achievements confirms rather than challenges stereotypical conceptions of Scottishness – may yet turn out to be something of an albatross, especially when set alongside the failure of other main-stage productions to repeat its success. Although it was originally conceived as a site-specific work, the key measures of the success of *Black Watch* have been the number of overseas venues to which it has travelled, the number of overseas critics it has wowed and the number of overseas awards it has received. It is these achievements that are foregrounded on the NTS website (www.nationaltheatreofscotland.com) and that have been consistently celebrated in the wider Scottish media.

For the NTS in particular – since it has been charged with the responsibility of representing the nation at home and abroad – but arguably for all theatre practitioners working in twenty-first-century Scotland, striking a productive balance between national and international engagements, and between inclusive and exclusive conceptions of Scottish identity, continues to be a live challenge. This balancing is in turn related to wider discourses of identity politics in contemporary Scotland. The decades leading up to devolution included two events that impacted the renegotiation of the idea of Scotland on a number of levels: the failure of the devolutionary project in March 1979, and the election later the same year of a UK Conservative government under Margaret Thatcher. Largely because of the 40 per cent rule imposed by Westminster, the outcome of the 1979 referendum left many in Scotland feeling cheated, but perhaps more tellingly Thatcher's brand of neo-liberal conservatism proved a political philosophy profoundly at odds with the values of Scottish civic society. One consequence of this fundamental tension was that during the 1980s Scottishness as a marker of identity became increasingly synonymous with hostility to Thatcher's free-market neo-nationalism. Consequently, the decade witnessed a collapse in the Conservative vote in Scotland from which it has never recovered. McCrone notes, for example, that between 1979 and 1997 the Conservative share of the vote among the high-earning Scottish professional and managerial classes – the party's natural constituency – dropped from 46 per cent to 23 per cent (*Understanding Scotland*, p. 122). Scotland, and in particular its relationship to England, had changed.

Identities: fixed and fluid

Far from snuffing out creativity, Thatcherism – by throwing into stark relief the perceived differences between Scotland and England in terms of social values – provided the impetus for artistic endeavour. Steve Cramer, in his chapter 'The Traverse, 1985–97' (2011), shows, for example, how the Edinburgh theatre responded creatively to 'Thatcherite arts policies' by launching in 1985 a 'radical new writing programme' that engaged directly with and openly attacked 'the forms of ideological myth that had sustained Thatcherism thus far' (p. 165). This 1985 season, which included work by Peter Arnott, Jo Clifford and Chris Hannan, is now seen as a pivotal moment in the resurgence of Scottish theatre and as paving the way for the emergence of a new generation of internationally successful Scottish playwrights in the 1990s. Of this newer group, which includes David Harrower, Anthony Neilson and later Gregory Burke, David Greig has proven perhaps the most significant, and certainly the most prolific. In the discussion that follows, the work of these playwrights will be examined in relation to the ways in which it reflects and inflects contemporary conceptions of Scottish identity. In the conclusion, mention will also be made of a number of leading theatre companies whose work has extended the vocabulary through which Scottish performance culture engages with these identity politics. Although restrictions on space prohibit extended analyses of particular performances or theatre makers, my intention is to capture some sense of the vitality and variety of Scotland's contemporary theatre scene.

As an independent dramatist and founding member of the influential performance company Suspect Culture, David Greig has repeatedly, if sometimes obliquely, explored the scope and direction of Scotland's engagement with local, European and global contexts. In major plays such as *Europe* (Traverse, 1995), *The Cosmonaut's Last Message to the Woman He Once Loved in the Former Soviet Union* (Paines Plough, 1999) and *Pyrenees* (Paines Plough, 2005), he has complicated and problematised notions of 'essential Scottishness', preferring to stage what David Pattie, in a chapter titled 'Scotland & Anywhere' (2011), describes as 'identity fundamentally in relation, fundamentally linked to and in dialogue with all other identities that surround and inform it' (p. 57). Among other things, Greig's transnational focus, which is explored extensively in Muller and Wallace's *Cosmotopia*, has meant that when Scottish characters take centre stage in his work they are often displaced or marginalised, their sense of identity figured as unstable or vexed. It is perhaps surprising, then, that at the end of the first decade of the new millennium Greig turned his hand to a history play that takes medieval Scotland as its setting.

Commissioned by the RSC in 2010 and revived the following year in a co-production with the NTS, *Dunsinane* looks both inward, towards Scotland's past, and outward to comment on twenty-first-century global politics. In this way it embodies the tension between national and international concerns explored in the previous section. Possibly best described as a revisionist sequel to *Macbeth*, the play begins in the middle of the battle that signals the final defeat of the tyrant and follows the fortunes of the English army and their commander, Siward, as they attempt to facilitate Malcolm's restoration. The medieval Scotland evoked by Greig is a harsh and mythical place, a country – it is strongly implied – too subtle, multifaceted and geographically hostile ever to be understood or conquered by the English. It is also a country divided by shifting tribal allegiances. Malcolm's return is not universally welcomed, and Scotland remains stubbornly hostile to the English interlopers who accompany him. Macbeth's widow – her historical name, Gruach, restored – has not conveniently succumbed to madness and suicide but instead lives on, as does a fifteen-year-old son from an earlier marriage, providing focus for dissent. Try as they might, the English cannot understand Scotland, its people, its customs, its landscape or its language. Instead they long for home, for 'lovely oak woods where everything is sun-dappled and the forests are full of wild boar and deer' (p. 51). As the action progresses, the upright but inflexible Siward is figured as increasingly out of place and out of his depth, his failure to understand the host culture evident both in his inability to comprehend the indigenous language – it is significant that he makes no attempt to learn it – and in his failure to appreciate the subtlety and complexity of

Scotland's political landscape. Eventually his stubborn belief in the righteousness of his cause leads him to butchery. 'You're a good man Siward,' observes Gruach in the play's final scene. 'It would have been better if you weren't. There would have been much less blood' (p. 137).

Obviously Greig's title deliberately conjures up Shakespeare's *Macbeth*, and *Dunsinane*'s meanings are therefore substantially inter-textual, relying as they do on our familiarity with the older text. That said, insofar as it figures tyranny as a product of propaganda rather than deeds, and attacks the politics of benevolent imperialist intervention, *Dunsinane* functions powerfully as contemporary political allegory. 'Imagine', observed Michael Billington in a review in *The Guardian* on 18 February 2010, 'an inhospitable terrain full of powerful warlords and an occupying army aching to get home' (p. 36). Greig's critique of contemporary Western foreign policy is obvious, then, and the folly of attempting to establish peace through war is succinctly exposed in the play's action and in Malcolm's observation to Siward that 'You can no more force peace into existence than you can wander across the surface of the sea stamping the waves flat' (p. 126).

It is a marker of the subtlety of Greig's text and the shifting landscape of UK politics that *Dunsinane* read differently north of the border. On its first outing the RSC's publicity department envisioned it straightforwardly as Siward's play, as 'a vision of one man's attempt to restore peace in a country ravaged by war' (www.rsc.org.uk/whats-on/dunsinane), and English critics, following Billington, tended to read it primarily as a contemporary allegory. In Scotland, however, in the wake of the election of a majority Nationalist government, *Dunsinane* seemed as much about the occupied as the occupier. Perhaps most crucially, it appeared to be describing cultures so fundamentally different that self-governance and self-determination for each was not only desirable but also natural and inevitable. As the action of the play progresses and the political situation worsens, questions of dis-engagement take precedence, and in the end the important question for Siward is how to get out. 'There is a dance of leaving,' Gruach informs him pointedly. 'Try to learn the steps' (p. 78).

The idea that tensions between Scottish and English cultural values are irresolvable has gained ground in recent years among Scotland's left-of-centre progressive majority, as evidenced by the election in 2011 of a majority SNP government. Greig himself was among a group of prominent Scottish writers asked by *The Observer* on 28 August 2011 to respond to the question 'Scotland and England: What Future for the Union?' Describing himself as an 'old-fashioned social democrat', he explained that while instinctively disinclined towards nationalism, equating it 'with racism, xenophobia, inward-looking-ness and militarism', he has become increasingly convinced that a weakening of the Union is inevitable:

> If the Union between Scotland and England has been a marriage, then the Holyrood election was like the moment when the wife looks at her

husband and realises – suddenly and clearly – that it's over ... at the moment I expect I will vote for independence. I think a majority of Scots will too. Perhaps not independence red in tooth and claw. Perhaps independence 'lite' ... but I don't think there's any going back. (p. 18)

In the same article Greig acknowledges that his misgivings about nationalism have been assuaged partly by the inclusive rhetoric of the SNP, which in the past decade has campaigned consistently for increased immigration and for a progressive social agenda, claiming much of the centre-left ground previously occupied by the Labour Party. Speaking to the Scottish Parliament on the occasion of his re-appointment as First Minister on 18 May 2011, the leader of the SNP, Alex Salmond, offered a seductively inclusive definition of Scottishness:

When Donald Dewar addressed this parliament in 1999, he evoked Scotland's diverse voices: the speak of the Mearns; the shout of the welder above the din of the Clyde shipyard; the battle cries of Bruce and Wallace. Now these voices of the past are joined in this chamber by the sound of 21st century Scotland: the lyrical Italian of Marco Biagi; the formal Urdu of Humza Yousaf; the sacred Arabic of Hanzala Malik. We are proud to have those languages spoken here alongside English, Gaelic, Scots and Doric. This

> land is their land, from the sparkling sands of
> the islands to the glittering granite of its cities. It
> belongs to all who choose to call it home.

There is, of course, a world of difference between employing inclusive rhetoric and creating a genuinely inclusive society, and it would be disingenuous to imply that Scotland has somehow been transformed by devolution into a utopian and egalitarian space. In reality Scotland, like the rest of Britain, remains a stubbornly unequal society, as the 2010 report from the Equality and Human Rights Commission in Scotland listed in the further reading shows.

Nonetheless, the idea of Scotland as a nation that might comfortably accommodate multiple or even contradictory identities is an attractive one for many, theatre makers included. Perhaps unsurprisingly, it has been a feature of work emerging from Scotland's immigrant communities. Marcella Evaristi's *Commedia* (Crucible Theatre, Sheffield, 1982), for instance, tells the story of Elena, a fifty-two-year-old Scots-Italian widow, who travels from Glasgow to Bologna and back, ostensibly in pursuit of a love affair but ultimately in a quest to reconcile her own dual identity, which emerges as both Scottish and Italian. Similarly, Ann Marie Di Mambro's *Tally's Blood* (Traverse, 1990), which has become a standard text in Scottish schools, shifts location between Scotland and Italy. Covering the period 1936–1955, it tells the story of the Pedreschi family and the racism they encounter as Italian immigrants in Scotland in the run-up to and the aftermath of the Second World War.

In Di Mambro's play questions around the desirability and possibility of integration are explored via tensions between Rosinella and Massimo, the husband and wife at the centre of the action. Rosinella's fierce commitment to her Italian identity manifests in a series of racist slurs against her Scottish neighbours, and although the tone of the dialogue is largely comic, the potentially problematic relationship between nationalist politics and racism is nevertheless spotlighted. It is only after a return visit to Italy that Rosinella is awakened to the potential benefits in embracing the Scottish part of her identity. More recently Matthew Zajac's *The Tailor of Inverness* (Dogstar, 2008) explores the ambiguities inherent in sustaining more than one identity by making use of his Polish father's personal history as a soldier, migrant and refugee during and after the Second World War. Also peeking from the periphery, geographically speaking, the Caithness playwright Henry Adam offers re-imaginings of what might constitute family, community and a sense of belonging in the twenty-first century. In *The People Next Door* (Traverse, 2003), for example, Nigel, a mixed-race British Asian, Marco, a disaffected black teenager, and Mrs Mac, an elderly Scottish widow, form an unlikely alliance in the face of institutional paranoia following 9/11.

As well as giving voice to the experience of immigrant communities, *Commedia* and *Tally's Blood* evidence the increasing presence of a female voice on a Scottish stage hitherto and even now largely dominated by masculine voices and concerns. Scottish theatre is not particularly unusual in this bias, of course. While it is not the purpose of this volume to critique the power structures that marginalise women in the British theatre, it might be noted that of the twenty-five essays recently published as *The Methuen Drama Guide to Contemporary British Playwrights* (2011) only seven are devoted to female playwrights, one of whom – Sarah Kane – is dead. In specifically Scottish terms such gender bias is not peculiar to the stage but rather reflects the pre-occupations of Scottish culture in general. As we have seen, the iconography of Scottishness has historically been dominated by masculine imagery, particularly that of the soldier and the skilled manual worker. Thankfully, these monolithic constructions can be, and have been, challenged. As Tom Maguire notes in his chapter 'Women Playwrights from the 1970s and 1980s' (2011), Scotland's female dramatists, building on the achievements of Ena Lamont Stewart, have 'helped reveal new dimensions to Scotland as imaginative space', making significant contributions to extending not only the subject matter and settings of Scottish drama, but its formal dimensions (p. 159). These playwrights have not found it easy to make their voices heard, however, and as Maguire points out, it is 'no small irony' that two of Scotland's most successful women dramatists, Rona Munro and Sharman Macdonald, have relied on close associations with theatres in England to support their work (p. 156).

Alongside Liz Lochhead, whose poetic dramas and translations into Scots have achieved critical and popular success, Rona Munro has emerged as an important figure. Coming to real prominence and winning the *Evening Standard* Most Promising Playwright Award with *Bold Girls* (7:84, 1991), which tells the story of three Belfast women against the backdrop of the Troubles, Munro has focused substantially although not exclusively on female experience in her work. Moreover, she regularly presses at the boundaries of realism to reveal the internal or hidden lives of her characters. In *Your Turn to Clean the Stairs* (Traverse, 1992), for instance, sections of the action occur in a kind of expressionistic dream state, and in her earliest work, *Fugue* (Traverse, 1982), the central character Kay's split personality is externalised as two actresses compete for control of her psyche. In addition to questioning the efficacy of realism as a mode for representing female experience, women playwrights have drawn on mythic and folkloric elements to critique historically determined patriarchal constructions of femininity. Sue Glover's *The Seal Wife* (Little Lyceum, Edinburgh, 1980) uses the legend of the selkies, or seal-people, to explore the domestic restrictions placed on women in a coastal village in southern Fife. According to legend, the seal-wife would transform herself into human form, marry and bear children, only to return to the sea at some later date. Glover's protagonist, Rona, dissatisfied with her role as wife and mother, eventually abandons her family. In the play Glover transforms the selkie legend from a narrative of deceit into one of resistance to the claustrophobic restrictions of patriarchy. Similarly, Munro's *The Maiden Stone* (Hampstead Theatre, London, 1995), set in her native northeast in the early part of the nineteenth century, draws on and inverts local myths of chastity, in the process attacking the demonisation of female sexuality that characterises patriarchal ideology. In *The Last Witch* (EIF, 2009), Munro returned to Sutherland for a fictional account of the life of Janet Horne, who in 1727 became the last women to be burned as a witch in Scotland. Set in the village of Dornoch, *The Last Witch* imagines Janet as a strong, wilful and eccentric fantasist, and the superstitious and claustrophobic community that turns on her as profoundly misogynistic. As Lyn Gardner observes in *The Guardian*, in this fictionalised account, the devil 'appears in many guises, but all of them male' (25 August 2009, p. 8). Again, the expression of female sexual desire – for Janet is free with her favours – provokes a disproportionally violent response.

Scotland's female dramatists have also taken the lead in extending the range of possible settings in theatre, moving beyond the domestic and workplace interiors of urban Scotland. The narrative of Sharman Macdonald's *When I Was a Girl I Used to Scream and Shout* (Bush, London, 1984) unfolds largely on an east coast beach, as does Glover's *The Seal Wife*. Glover's award-winning *Bondagers* (Traverse, 1991) relates a year in the life of a group of nineteenth-century female farm labourers in the Borders, while her *Shetland Saga* (Traverse, 2000) is set in Lerwick. As well as expanding the imagined space of contemporary Scotland, these marginal – and in the case of beaches, liminal – settings often reflect the emotional realities of central characters. In *When We Were Women* (National Theatre, London, 1988), as well as in *When I Was a Girl*, Macdonald explores discourses surrounding child bearing, abortion and marriage, primarily through the prism of mother/daughter relationships. While her characters are often successful and independent, they are typically emotionally and spiritually unfulfilled, seeking to recapture or revisit childhood innocence in order to more fully understand the present. These themes of displacement, marginalisation and isolation recur in Scottish women's drama, as does a tendency to explore these issues in personal terms and in specific localities.

Zinnie Harris's *Further Than the Furthest Thing* (Tron Theatre, Glasgow, and National Theatre, 2000) begins on a remote island in the middle of the South Atlantic, a fictionalised version of the British territory Tristan da Cunha. The first act ends with a volcanic eruption, a cataclysmic event that triggers the evacuation of the islanders to Southampton, the setting for the second act. Harris uses various external markers – dress, custom and especially language – to construct the island community as culturally specific and 'other'. At the mercy of environmental and colonial forces outside their control and understanding, the islanders spend much of the second act longing for a return to their native shores, which they finally achieve. It may be because of its history as a migrant nation that the pull of native shores is a prevalent motif across Scottish culture – most typically figured in narratives featuring the return of soldiers or economic migrants. At any rate, this motif persists in contemporary drama, and not just drama by women, featuring in one form or another in Stephen Greenhorn's *The Salt Wound* (7:84, 1994), David Harrower's *Kill the Old Torture Their Young* (Traverse, 1998) and Suspect Culture's *Casanova* (2001), for example.

Much of the work described above complicates the idea of a stable and coherent Scottish body politic by focusing on the marginalised, on outsiders and the periphery. While they have arguably taken the lead, female playwrights have not been alone in exploring this territory. An increased focus on the politics of inclusion and exclusion, on lives lived on borders, sometimes looking in and sometimes looking out, and on communities as claustrophobic and oppressive as well as inclusive has been apparent elsewhere. In particular, David Harrower's work is marked by a persistent ambivalence about the possibility of shared values. His debut, *Knives in Hens* (Traverse, 1995), is a compelling and subtle exploration of how patriarchal power relations are enforced through language. Set in an ill-defined pre-industrial past and in no recognisable country, it features, as Steve Cramer notes, a 'young woman so oppressed by patriarchal language she remains nameless' ('The Traverse, 1985–97', p. 172). In performance, *Knives in Hens* is an intensely lyrical and atmospheric play. An explication of its plot does little to communicate its power. The many failures in communication that characterise its bleak poetry create a sense of characters irrevocably trapped in their own realities, and while the young woman eventually escapes the clutches of an oppressive husband, by joining forces with her lover to murder him, the exact significance of this event remains ambiguous. The young woman acquires agency via her encounter with the socially marginalised miller Gilbert Cross, who later becomes her lover – or more specifically via a passion for the written word that Cross reignites in her. In this sense *Knives in Hens* might be read as a narrative of enlightenment and liberation. However, Harrower's linking of knowledge, specifically female knowledge, with violence and deceit, as Clare Wallace observes in her chapter on the playwright's work in *The Methuen Drama Guide to Contemporary British Playwrights*, 'inevitably suggests the fall of man' and is consequently somewhat problematic (p. 248). In the play's ambiguous resolution, the young woman decides to remain in the village playing the grieving widow, while the miller leaves:

Gilbert I want more. In the town there's books and pens and paper. Owned by people who've left villages. They speak all day about everything in the world. (p. 39)

Because of its powerful poetic appeal, and perhaps also because of its lack of geographical or temporal specificity, *Knives in Hens* has been widely produced internationally, as has Harrower's Olivier-winning *Blackbird* (EIF, 2005), which began life in a production by the influential German director Peter Stein. If *Knives in Hens* is unsettling in its ambivalence, *Blackbird* is disturbingly so. In the play Una, a woman in her late twenties, confronts Peter, a man in his mid-fifties, in an anonymous litter-strewn staff common room. It quickly becomes apparent that the two had a sexual relationship fifteen years earlier, when she was twelve and he was around forty, which resulted in Peter serving a three-year prison sentence. Una, it transpires, has tracked Peter down after seeing his picture in a trade magazine. At one level *Blackbird* is a conventionally realist play about the impact of the past on the present. However, as Wallace notes, because it 'sustains an acute level of ambivalence' in dealing with its controversial subject matter, its effects are compelling and unsettling (p. 254). Most significantly, Una's exact motivation for confronting Peter is never clear. Does she want to accuse him, to humiliate him, to attack him, to extract an apology or to rekindle their sexual relationship?

In *Blackbird*, the boundaries between moral categories are blurred because the adult Una is a damaged and destructive presence and therefore not easily recognised as a victim. In addition, the implication that their earlier sexual relationship was in some meaningful sense consensual is given some credence. In the absence of an actual child onstage, the audience is left to imagine the twelve-year-old Una, who is constructed, as Wallace observes, 'as endowed with adult agency and self-aware sexuality, while Peter's responsibility as an adult *not* to respond is obscured by the assertion of consensual love' (p. 256). Harrower's intensity of focus, his expertly written dialogue and his sustained ambivalence, especially around the figure of Una, compromise the audience's ability to develop a stable perspective from which to interpret the narrative ethically, forcing them to ask uncomfortable questions about the boundaries between love, abuse and sexual consent. This is quite an achievement given that most people understand clearly that it is morally reprehensible for a forty-year-old man to have sex with a twelve-year-old girl.

Like *Knives in Hens*, *Blackbird* does not seem geographically or culturally specific. It focuses instead on individuals isolated within subjective realities. In this sense both plays can be considered genuinely antisocial. For Cramer this absence, or relegation, of social context as a determinant of human behaviour is a defining feature of Harrower's work, which, he argues, is informed by 'the post-Thatcher era's extreme paranoia and individualist ethos' (p. 173). Similar arguments might be staged about Anthony Neilson, whose plays since the 1990s have been remarkable for their consistent privileging of subjective over objective realities. John Bull, in *The Methuen Drama Guide to Contemporary British Playwrights*, has aptly described Neilson's political impulse, if indeed he can be said to have one, as 'towards individual anarchism' (p. 360). Neilson is unusual among contemporary Scottish dramatists in that his work achieved prominence in the 1990s as part of what Aleks Sierz labelled the 'in-yer-face' school. His inclusion in Sierz's *Decades of Modern British Playwriting: The 1990s* (2012) alongside Philip Ridley, Mark Ravenhill and Sarah Kane confirms his status as a major figure in the London-centred theatre of that decade. More recently, Neilson has moved away from a 'new brutalist' aesthetic to produce more formally experimental works such as *The Wonderful World of Dissocia* (Tron and EIF, 2004), *Realism* (NTS and EIF, 2006) and *Relocated* (Royal Court, 2008). In these plays Neilson continues to privilege felt experience over culturally imposed notions of 'normality' by staging – in a cocktail of memory, fantasy, nightmare and reality – the insides of his characters' heads. His focus on the marginalised individual subject, combined with an almost complete absence of reference to contemporary

Scottish political debates, means that Neilson's work, like Harrower's, provides a sustained challenge to – or at least succeeds in qualifying – reductive or essentialist constructions of Scottish identity. However, this is not to imply that contemporary Scottish theatre as a whole has avoided overt engagement with issues of national identity or abandoned its existing iconography.

Since his debut, *Gagarin Way* (Traverse, 2001), Gregory Burke has produced plays that privilege masculine ways of knowing, in the process focusing substantially on the experiences of working-class men. In *Gagarin Way* self-educated factory worker Eddie and his accomplice Gary, a disillusioned political activist, kidnap Frank, a visiting factory manager, in what proves to be a futile and violent act of resistance against the vagaries of global capitalism. In *The Straits* (Paines Plough, 2003), set among the families of the British military in Gibraltar during the Falklands War, the teenager Darren is able to achieve acceptance among the British community only through violence, and in *Black Watch*, as we have seen, Burke reinvigorates and reanimates the iconography of the Scottish soldier to paint a picture of a masculine community established through centuries of shared experience: 'We're a fucking tribe ourselves' (p. 31).

Burke's only significant attempt to write female characters, in *Hoors* (Traverse, 2009), provoked a lukewarm critical response, leading *The Observer*'s Euan Ferguson to wonder, for instance, whether the playwright's 'often wonderful words work better in the mouths of men' (10 May 2009, p. 15). Unlike most of his contemporaries, Burke retains a masculinist focus, regularly revisiting the themes of Scottish drama of the 1970s, especially the negative effects wrought by the decline of heavy industry on the working-class male psyche. The powerlessness of working men in the face of larger economic forces was a prominent theme in Bill Bryden's *Willie Rough* (Lyceum, 1972), for instance, in Billy Connolly and Tom Buchan's *The Great Northern Welly Boot Show* (Glasgow Fair International, 1972) and in much of the work of 7:84 (Scotland). It is noticeable that Burke's work, while often compelling, consistently fails to problematise its own residual masculinism – that is, the grounds on which it constructs and critiques the world from an exclusively masculine perspective. In this, Burke's plays can be usefully located within a tradition described by Christopher Whyte, in 'Masculinities in Contemporary Scottish Fiction' (1998), in which the prominence of the 'hard man' signals that the work 'of embodying and transmitting Scottishness is, as it were, devolved to the unemployed, the socially under-privileged' and, most importantly, the working-class male (p. 275). It is also interesting that David Pattie, in his recent account of Burke's work in *The Methuen Drama Guide to Contemporary British Playwrights*, chooses to analyse the plays from within this tradition, ignoring feminist or post-colonial perspectives. For Pattie, critiques of *Black Watch* that 'take it to task for missing out part of the history of the regiment, or for ignoring the plight of ordinary Iraqi's, rather miss the point'. Instead, Pattie argues, Burke's plays should be understood as 'primarily about the effects on people when apparently rooted, immutable institutions disappear' (p. 35). Burke's limited construction of the nation in *Black Watch* – in his introduction to the text he identifies 'soldiering' as 'arguably the only significant indigenous industry to have lasted into the twenty first century' – is mirrored in Pattie's use of the word 'people' to mean men (p. viii). In both cases, as Gerard Carruthers, David Goldie and Alastair Renfrew have argued in their introduction to *Beyond Scotland* (2004), such constructions run the risk of deforming the idea of Scottishness by replacing 'a complex, forward-looking, heterogeneous identity' with 'one that is narrow and reductive in its nativism' (p. 15).

Conclusion

In the present as in the past, those who believe Scottish culture is being eroded, or who lack confidence in the ability of Scotland to persist, seek essentialist definitions of Scottishness that do not stand up to close scrutiny, and work to freeze the culture rather than allowing scope for variation and development. Writing in *The Scotsman* in November 1997, after the referendum that led to the establishment of the Scottish Parliament, David Harrower and David Greig argued for the post-devolutionary Scottish stage as a site of cultural transformation:

> Scotland has voted to redefine itself as a nation. To redefine ourselves we need to understand ourselves, exchange ideas and aspirations, confront enduring myths, expose injustices, and explore our past. The quality, accessibility,

and immediacy of Scottish theatre make it one of the best arenas in which these dialogues can take place. ('Why a New Scotland Must Have a Properly Funded Theatre', p. 15)

Broadly speaking, Scottish theatre has risen admirably to this challenge. As this short account demonstrates, dramatists such as Adam, Burke, Glover, Greig, Harris, Harrower, Munro and Neilson, by engaging with a wide range of discourses of identity, including class, gender, ethnicity and multiculturalism, have insisted that if the notion of an inclusive and heterogeneous Scotland is to be taken seriously, the country must carefully consider how such positive ambitions are to be culturally animated and not simply take them for granted. Scotland's theatre artists have made a significant contribution to establishing what might be seen as a conceptual infrastructure for the culture of a future Scotland with democratic control of its own affairs. In particular, since 2006 the now centrally funded NTS has produced work largely focused on contemporary Scotland rather than the past. In September 2011 the Scottish government announced that revenue funding for the NTS would remain stable in 2012/13. Unfortunately, smaller theatre companies have not fared as well. From 2013, Creative Scotland will receive less money from the Scottish government and more from lottery funds (which, it should be remembered, cannot be spent on core funding but only on specified projects). The controversial result of this change is that a number of internationally acclaimed Scottish performance companies, including

Glasgow's Vanishing Point and Edinburgh's Grid Iron, will now be obliged to apply for funding on a project-to-project basis. This is particularly disappointing because the vocabulary of Scottish theatre has been vastly enriched since the 1990s by a new generation of Scottish performance companies that exemplify, perhaps more than any other aspect of Scotland's performance culture, the country's new-found confidence and engagement with international discourses of postmodernism and globalisation. Companies such as Suspect Culture, Theatre Cryptic, Grid Iron and Vanishing Point have arguably been most successful in embodying the multifaceted, outward-looking and heterogeneous landscape of contemporary Scotland.

Beginning in the early 1990s, Suspect Culture – actor/director Graham Eatough, playwright David Greig, composer/musician Nick Powell and designer Ian Scott – created a series of works in collaboration with artists in Scotland and continental Europe that established them as Scotland's leading company in this area. Initially, their work stood out because of its thematic concerns: its focus on a twenty-something generation wandering through a landscape of globalisation distinguished it from the earlier Scottish tradition of direct political engagement. As Dan Rebellato points out in his 2003 article ' "And I Will Reach Out My Hand with a Kind of Infinite Slowness and Say the Perfect Thing": The Utopian Theatre of Suspect Culture', the cool intellectualism of their work also divided critics, as did their commitment to formal experimentation. In *Mainstream* (1999) – a melancholy meditation on a sexual encounter between a music business executive and a per-sonnel consultant – the couple was played by four actors appearing and reappearing in all available combinations, revisiting, revising and re-voicing conversations so that it soon became very difficult to recall who had said what to whom. The difficulty, or even impossibility, of sustained meaningful communication between individuals in an advanced commodity culture was thus embedded in the show at the level of its structure. *Lament* (2002) began with projections of video footage of interviews with the performers. In deceptively relaxed and informal style, they recalled childhood memories, favourite outfits, present-day problems and detailed fantasies about their ideal futures. This material was then playfully transcribed into the fabric of the remainder of the show, with performers appearing in the clothes they had previously described and recycling phrases used by their on-screen selves. Many of the short overlapping scenes that made up the remainder of the piece circulated around the characters' fantasies as described by their video personas. Importantly, the audience was given no reliable means of gauging the veracity of the characters' testimonies. In this way, the show became a lament for the kinds of lives people should or could have lived instead of the ones they were actually living. Suspect Culture con-tinued to produce innovative and thought-provoking work, often marked by a sophisticated visual style and ensemble playing, into the new century, finally disbanding in 2009. It was not the only experimental company to emerge in the 1990s.

Having moved from her native Belfast to study in Glasgow in 1990, Cathie Boyd founded Theatre Cryptic in 1994 and has gone on to direct a number of visually stunning and award-winning shows, including *Bonjour Tristesse* (1995), *Prologue* (1998), *Trojan Women* (2005) and *Orlando* (2010). Many of Cryptic's shows feature original scores and live musicians – the company also creates sonic installations – and their theatre work is distinguished by a highly visual style (www.theatrecryptic.org.uk). Joyce MacMillan's review of *Orlando* in *The Scotsman* gives a flavour of the work:

> the extraordinary visual images and effects by James Houston and Angelica Kroeger...reach a climax in the long central sequence of liquid light and shimmering outlines through which Orlando makes her transition from one sex to the other. The overall effect is dazzling; and so rich in texture, and in the layers of meaning surrounding this remarkable story, that it demands to be seen not once, but many times; and each time, I suspect, with more feeling. (1 October 2010, p. 15)

With the stated aim of producing work that ravishes the senses and fuses music, dance, sonic art and multimedia, Theatre Cryptic has internationalism at its heart, performing as far afield as the Belfast Festival, BITE at the Barbican, the Divadlo Festival in the Czech Republic, the Edinburgh International Festival and the Singapore Arts Festival.

Glasgow is also home to Vanishing Point, a company formed in 1999 by Matthew Lenton. Like Cryptic, Vanishing Point produces visually stunning work that combines a range of media and art forms (www.vanishing-point.org). Lenton, who has directed all of the company's work to date, has shown a particular interest in European texts and aesthetics, creating *Little Otik* (2009), inspired by the film of the same name by cult surrealist Czech animator Jan Švankmajer, and adapting Maurice Maeterlinck's late nineteenth-century symbolist dramas *Les Aveugles* and *Intérieur* as *The Sightless* (1999) and *Interiors* (2009). The influence of European modernism is also apparent in Lenton's stated ambition to turn the stage into a space 'that is otherworldly, magical and atmospheric'. Elsewhere, under the direction of Ben Harrison, Edinburgh-based Grid Iron has emerged as Scotland's leading site-specific company. Harrison's award-winning production of Douglas Maxwell's breakthrough play *Decky Does a Bronco* (Grid Iron, 2000) was performed in a children's playground and explored the brutality and intensity of childhood experience. Set in Girvan, on the west coast of Scotland, in the summer of 1983, the play examines how proficiency in playground stunts becomes a marker of status for a gang of nine-year-old boys, with tragic-comic rwesults. In Harrison's site-specific production adult male performers switched between childhood experience and adult reflection in a way that spotlighted dislocations in the construction and maintenance of stable adult identity under pressure from forces of memory and guilt. In April 2006, in a co-production with the newly established

NTS, Grid Iron used Edinburgh International airport as the site for *Roam*, a meditation on the mass movement of people across borders that involved an international cast and a large group of amateur performers, including children and the elderly. Utilising the various spaces of the airport after the departure of the last flight, *Roam* reflected on identity issues in national and international contexts. It focused on the inequalities that characterise global capitalism, on the war on terror, and on aviation, and thus technology, as a site of human achievement. More recently, *What Remains* (EIF, 2011) took the form of a promenade musical installation at Edinburgh University's School of Anatomy.

The blurring of boundaries between theatre, performance, dance, music and installation art that is apparent in Grid Iron's work features to a greater or lesser degree in the work of all the performance companies mentioned above. Their critical and commercial success is important because it serves to re-emphasise the heterogeneity of Scotland's performance culture. This heterogeneity, which is partly produced by Scotland's unusual performance history, is a particular and crucial strength especially in the post-devolutionary moment, when a redefining and re-imagining of Scottish identity in UK and European contexts is under way. For centuries Scottish culture was viewed as essentially anti-theatrical and dour. My aim in this book has been to challenge such preconceptions and in so doing to emphasise the extent to which contemporary Scottish theatre plays a significant role, though one foreshadowed in earlier periods, in expressing the multivalent, playful and performative nature of Scottish culture and identity. As a case study, Scotland is illuminating because its theatre, culture and politics have come significantly to benefit and prosper under the auspices of a new global zeitgeist suspicious of neat entities. Contemporary Scottish theatre makers remain conscious that processes of seeming cultural disintegration – such as the weakening of the Union – can be crucial in enabling democratic diversification.

further reading

The first port of call for anyone interested in Scottish theatre should be Ian Brown's edited collection *The Edinburgh Companion to Scottish Drama* (2011), which provides the most up-to-date survey of the field, including the kind of detailed coverage of the eighteenth- and nineteenth-century theatre that is missing from the present volume. The various attempts during that period to establish a legitimate and commercial theatre in Scotland, including those of the eighteenth-century Edinburgh actor-manager Allan Ramsay, have not been a focus of this book because I have chosen to foreground popular traditions and their impact on contemporary practice. These attempts are nevertheless important and significant, and you will find mention of them in general histories such as Bill Findlay's *A History of Scottish Theatre* (1998) and Donald Campbell's *Playing for Scotland* (1996). Similarly, James Bridie's important contribution at the Glasgow Citizens in the mid-twentieth century is covered both in the *Edinburgh Companion* and in Winifred Bannister's *James Bridie and His Theatre* (1955).

Paul Maloney's work on popular forms is always illuminating and thorough. In particular, his *Scotland and the Music Hall, 1850–1914* (2003) is a prodigiously researched and persuasively argued account of how the history of the halls in Scotland can add to our understanding of discourses of class, nation and Empire in the late Victorian and Edwardian periods. There is also quite a bit of good writing on Scottish women playwrights. Alongside Tom Maguire's chapter, 'Women Playwrights from the 1970s and 1980s', in the *Edinburgh Companion*, a good starting point would be Adrienne Scullions's 'Contemporary Scottish Women Playwrights' in *The Cambridge Companion to Modern British Women Playwrights*, edited by Elaine Aston and Janelle Reinelt (2000). Liz Lochhead has received particular attention both as a poet and as a playwright, and Ksenija Horvat's 'Liz Lochhead' in the *Edinburgh Companion* is a useful introduction to her work as a dramatist and performance artist. Among contemporary playwrights, Gregory Burke, David Greig, David Harrower and Anthony Neilson have been most widely produced and praised, each securing a dedicated chapter in *The Methuen Drama Guide to Contemporary British Playwrights*, edited by Aleks Sierz, Martin Middeke and Peter Schnierer (2011). While four out of twenty-five entries might not seem excessive, the absence of a single Welsh or Northern Irish playwright in *The Methuen Drama Guide* further evidences the growing reputation of Scottish theatre in the European academy, as does the publication of Anja Muller and Clare Wallace's edited collection *Cosmotopia: Transnational Identities in David Greig's Theatre* (2011). Neilson's work is discussed in some detail in my own article 'Deformities of the Frame' (2007) and in my chapter 'Anthony Neilson' in Aleks Sierz's *Modern British Playwriting: The 1990s* (2012).

The arrival of the NTS provoked two dedicated articles – my own 'From Scenes Like These Old Scotia's Grandeur Springs' (2007) and Robert Leach's 'The Short Astonishing History of the National Theatre of Scotland' (2006) – both of which flesh out the history of the campaign for a national theatre company in Scotland and survey the early work of the newly established company. For wider discussions of contemporary Scottish culture David McCrone's seminal *Understanding Scotland: The Sociology of a Nation* (2001), now in its second edition, provides an excellent introduction and is lucidly written. Similarly, Tom Devine is now considered the pre-eminent historian of modern Scotland, and his books *The Scottish Nation* (2000), *Scotland's Empire* (2004) and *To the Ends of the Earth* (2011) will provide any interested reader with a clear narrative and detailed understanding of the forces that have shaped, and continue to shape, Scotland over the past several centuries. Lastly, Nadine Holdsworth's *Theatre & Nation* (2010), in this series, provides a concise and stimulating overview of ideas relating to theatre and nationalism in a wider context.

Agate, James. *Immoment Toys: A Survey of Light Entertainment on the London Stage, 1920–1943*. London: Jonathan Cape, 1945.

Althusser, Louis. *Essays on Ideology*. London: Verso, 1970.

Aston, Elaine, and Janelle Reinelt, eds. *The Cambridge Companion to Modern British Women Playwrights*. Cambridge: Cambridge UP, 2000.

Bannister, Winifred. *James Bridie and His Theatre*. London: Rockliff, 1955.

Bell, Barbara. 'The National Drama and the Nineteenth Century.' *The Edinburgh Companion to Scottish Drama*. Ed. Ian Brown. Edinburgh: Edinburgh UP, 2011. 47–59.

Billington, Michael. '*Dunsinane*, Theatre Review.' *The Guardian* 18 February 2010: 36.

Brown, Ian, ed. *The Edinburgh Companion to Scottish Drama*. Edinburgh: Edinburgh UP, 2011.

————. 'Plugged into History.' *Scottish Theatre since the Seventies*. Ed. Randall Stevenson and Gavin Wallace. Edinburgh: Edinburgh UP, 1996. 84–99.

————. 'Public and Private Performance: 1650–1800.' *The Edinburgh Companion to Scottish Drama*. Ed. Ian Brown. Edinburgh: Edinburgh UP, 2011. 22–40.

————, ed. *From Tartan to Tartanry: Scottish Culture, History and Myth*. Edinburgh: Edinburgh UP, 2010.

Bull, John. 'Anthony Neilson.' *The Methuen Drama Guide to Contemporary British Playwrights*. Ed. Aleks Sierz, Martin Middeke, and Peter Schnierer. London: Methuen, 2011. 243–62.

Burke, Gregory. *The National Theatre of Scotland's Black Watch*. London: Faber & Faber, 2007.

Campbell, Donald. *Playing for Scotland: A History of the Scottish Stage 1715–1965*. Edinburgh: Mercat, 1996.

Carpenter, Sarah. 'Scottish Drama until 1650.' *The Edinburgh Companion to Scottish Drama*. Ed. Ian Brown. Edinburgh: Edinburgh UP, 2011. 6–21.

Carruthers, Gerard, David Goldie, and Alastair Renfrew, eds. *Beyond Scotland: New Contexts for Scottish Literature*. Amsterdam and New York: Rodopi, 2004.

Corbett, John. 'Translated Drama in Scotland.' *The Edinburgh Companion to Scottish Drama*. Ed. Ian Brown. Edinburgh: Edinburgh UP, 2011. 95–106.

————. *Written in the Language of the Scottish Nation: A History of Literary Translation into Scots.* Clevedon, UK: Multilingual Matters, 1999.

Coveney, Michael. *The Citizens': 21 Years of the Glasgow Citizens' Theatre.* London: Nick Hern, 1990.

Craig, Cairns, ed. *The History of Scottish Literature.* Vol. 4. *The Twentieth Century.* Aberdeen: Aberdeen UP, 1988.

————. *The Modern Scottish Novel.* Edinburgh: Edinburgh UP, 1999.

————. 'Myths against History: Tartanry and Kailyard in 19th-Century Scottish Literature.' *Scotch Reels: Scotland in Cinema and Television.* Ed. Colin McArthur. London: British Film Institute, 1982. 7–16.

————. 'Scotland and Hybridity.' *Beyond Scotland: New Contexts for Scottish Literature.* Ed. Gerard Carruthers, David Goldie, and Alastair Renfrew. Amsterdam and New York: Rodopi, 2004. 229–53.

Cramer, Steve. 'The Traverse, 1985–97: Arnott, Clifford, Hannan, Harrower, Greig and Greenhorn.' *The Edinburgh Companion to Scottish Drama.* Ed. Ian Brown. Edinburgh: Edinburgh UP, 2011. 165–76.

Crawford, Iain. *Banquo on Thursdays: The Inside Story of 50 Years of the Edinburgh Festival.* Edinburgh: Goblinshead, 1997.

Davis, Leith, Ian Duncan, and Janet Sorensen, eds. *Scotland and the Borders of Romanticism.* Cambridge: Cambridge UP, 2004.

Devine, Tom. *To the Ends of the Earth: Scotland's Global Diaspora.* London: Allen Lane, 2011.

————. *Scotland's Empire.* London: Penguin, 2004.

————. *The Scottish Nation.* London: Penguin, 2000.

————. 'Thank Calvin for Great Scots Minds.' *The Times* 10 August 2009: 17.

Di Cenzo, Maria. *The Politics of Alternative Theatre in Britain, 1968–1990: The Case of 7:84 Scotland.* Cambridge: Cambridge UP, 1996.

D'Monté, Rebecca, and Graham Saunders, eds. *Cool Britannia? British Political Drama in the 1990s.* Basingstoke, UK: Palgrave Macmillan, 2007.

Edinburgh International Festival. 'Our Mission'. <www.eif.co.uk/about-festival/our-mission/our-mission>.

Emmerson, George. *A Social History of Scottish Dance*. Montreal and London: McGill-Queen's UP, 1972.

Equality and Human Rights Commission Scotland and the Office for Public Management. 'Significant Inequalities in Scotland: Identifying Significant Inequalities and Priorities for Action.' 2010. <www.equalityhumanrights.com/scotland/research-in-scotland/>.

Evans, Caroline. *Fashion at the Edge: Spectacle, Modernity and Deathliness*. New Haven, CT: Yale UP, 2003.

Faiers, Jonathan. *Tartan*. Oxford: Berg, 2008.

Ferguson, Euan. 'Hoors.' *The Observer* 10 May 2009: 15.

Findlay, Bill, ed. *Frae Ither Tongues: Essays on Translations into Scots*. Clevedon, UK: Multilingual Matters, 2004.

———. *A History of Scottish Theatre*. Edinburgh: Polygon, 1998.

———, ed. *Scottish People's Theatre: Plays by Glasgow Unity Writers*. Glasgow: Association for Scottish Literary Studies, 2008.

———. 'Talking in Tongues: Scottish Translations.' *Scottish Theatre since the Seventies*. Ed. Randall Stevenson and Gavin Wallace. Edinburgh: Edinburgh UP, 1996. 186–97.

Folorunso, Femi. 'Scottish Drama and the Popular Tradition.' *Scottish Theatre since the Seventies*. Ed. Randall Stevenson and Gavin Wallace. Edinburgh: Edinburgh UP, 1996. 176–85.

Gardner, Lyn. 'The Last Witch.' *The Guardian* 25 August 2009: 8.

Gifford, Douglas, and Dorothy McMillan, eds. *A History of Scottish Women's Writing*. Edinburgh: Edinburgh UP, 1997.

The Glasgow Harlequin Summer 1896.

Greig, David. *Dunsinane*. London: Faber & Faber, 2010.

———. *The Strange Undoing of Prudencia Hart*. London: Faber & Faber, 2011.

Greig, David, and Lluïsa Cunillé. *The Speculator/The Meeting*. London: Methuen, 1999.

Greig, David, et al. 'Scotland and England: What Future for the Union?' *The Observer*, 28 August 2011: 18.

Hague, Euan. 'The Scottish Diaspora: Tartan Day and the Appropriation of Scottish Identities in the United States.' *Celtic Geographies: Old Culture, New Times*. Ed. David Harvey, Rhys Jones, Neil McInroy, and Christine Milligan. London: Routledge, 2002. 139–56.

Harrower, David. *Knives in Hens*. London: Methuen, 1997.

Harrower, David, and David Greig. 'Why a New Scotland Must Have a Properly Funded Theatre.' *The Scotsman* 25 November 1997: 15.

Harvie, Christopher. *No Gods and Precious Few Heroes: Twentieth-Century Scotland*. London: Arnold, 1981.

Harvie, Jen. 'Cultural Effects of the Edinburgh International Festival: Elitism, Identities, Industries.' *Contemporary Theatre Review* 13.4 (2003): 12–26.

———. *Staging the UK*. Manchester: Manchester UP, 2005.

Holdsworth, Nadine. 'The Landscape of Contemporary Scottish Drama: Place, Politics and Identity.' *A Concise Companion to Contemporary British and Irish Drama*. Ed. Nadine Holdsworth and Mary Luckhurst. Malden, MA: Blackwell, 2008. 125–45.

———. *Theatre & Nation*. Basingstoke, UK: Palgrave Macmillan, 2010.

———. 'Travelling across Borders: Re-Imagining the Nation and Nationalism in Contemporary Scottish Theatre.' *Contemporary Theatre Review* 13.2 (2003): 25–39.

Hutchison, David. *The Modern Scottish Theatre*. Glasgow: Molendinar, 1977.

Kershaw, Baz. *The Politics of Performance: Radical Theatre As Cultural Intervention*. London: Routledge, 1992.

King, Elspeth. 'Popular Culture in Glasgow.' *The Working Class in Glasgow, 1750–1914*. Ed. R. A. Cage. London: Croom Helm, 1987. 142–87.

Klein, Naomi. *No Logo*. New York: Picador, 2000.

Lamont Stewart, Ena. 'Men Should Weep.' *Scottish People's Theatre: Plays by Glasgow Unity Writers*. Ed. Bill Findlay. Glasgow: Association of Scottish Literary Studies, 2008. 57–122.

Leach, Robert. 'The Short Astonishing History of the National Theatre of Scotland.' *New Theatre Quarterly* 23.2 (2006): 171–83.

Lochhead, Liz. *Miseryguts and Tartuffe: Two Plays by Molière*. London: Nick Hern, 2002.

MacDiarmid, Hugh. Letter. *Glasgow Herald* 4 February 1947.

——— 'Scottish People and Scotch Comedians.' *Stewartry Observer* 23 August 1928. [Written under the pseudonym 'Special Correspondent'.]

MacMillan, Joyce. 'Orlando.' *The Scotsman* 1 October 2010: 15.

Maguire, Tom. 'Women Playwrights from the 1970s and 1980s.' *The Edinburgh Companion to Scottish Drama*. Ed. Ian Brown. Edinburgh: Edinburgh UP, 2011. 154–64.

Maloney, Paul. 'Ethnic Representation in Popular Theatre.' *From Tartan to Tartanry: Scottish Culture, History and Myth*. Ed. Ian Brown. Edinburgh: Edinburgh UP, 2010. 129–50.

———. *Scotland and the Music Hall, 1850–1914*. Manchester: Manchester UP, 2003.

Martell, Luke. 'Britain and Globalization.' *Globalizations* 5.3 (2008): 449–66.

Mayer, David. 'Towards a Definition of Popular Drama.' *Western Popular Theatre*. Ed. David Mayer and Kenneth Richards. London: Methuen, 1997. 257–76.

McArthur, Colin. *Scotch Reels*. London: British Film Institute, 1982.

McCrone, David. *Understanding Scotland: The Sociology of a Nation*. 2nd ed. London: Routledge, 2001.

McGavin, John. *Theatricality and Narrative in Medieval and Early Modern Scotland: Studies in Performance and Early Modern Drama*. Aldershot, UK: Ashgate, 2007.

McGrath, John. *The Cheviot, the Stag and the Black, Black Oil*. London: Methuen, 1981.

———. *A Good Night Out: Popular Theatre, Class and Form*. London: Methuen, 1981.

Mill, Anna J. *Mediaeval Plays in Scotland*. St Andrews: St Andrew's U Publications, 1924.

Milne, Drew. 'Cheerful History: The Political Theatre of John McGrath.' *New Theatre Quarterly* 18.4 (2002): 313–24.

Moffat, Alasdair. *The Edinburgh Fringe*. London: Johnston & Bacon, 1988.

Monod, Paul, Murray Pittock, and Daniel Szechi, eds. *Loyalty and Identity: Jacobites at Home and Abroad*. Basingstoke, UK: Palgrave Macmillan, 2009.

Muller, Anja, and Clare Wallace, eds. *Cosmotopia: Transnational Identities in David Greig's Theatre*. Prague: Univerzita Karlova, 2011.

Nairn, Tom. *After Britain*. London: Granta, 2000.

———. *The Break-up of Britain*. London: New Left Books, 1977.

O'Donnell, Hugh. 'Class Warriors or Generous Men in Skirts?' *From Tartan to Tartanry: Scottish Culture, History and Myth*. Ed. Ian Brown. Edinburgh: Edinburgh UP, 2010. 212–31.

Pattie, David. 'Gregory Burke.' *The Methuen Drama Guide to Contemporary British Playwrights*. Ed. Aleks Sierz, Martin Middeke, and Peter Schnierer. London: Methuen, 2011. 22–41.

———. 'Mapping the Territory: Modern Scottish Drama.' *Cool Britannia? British Political Drama in the 1990s*. Ed. Rebecca D'Monté and Graham Saunders. Basingstoke, UK: Palgrave Macmillan, 2007. 143–57.

———. 'Scotland & Anywhere: The Theatre of David Greig.' *Cosmotopia: Transnational Identities in David Greig's Theatre*. Ed. Anja Muller and Clare Wallace. Prague: Univerzita Karlova, 2011. 50–65.

Peacock, Noel. *Molière in Scotland*. Glasgow: Glasgow UP, 1993.

Pittock, Murray. *The Myth of the Jacobite Clans*. Edinburgh: Edinburgh UP, 1995.

———. 'Plaiding the Invention of Scotland.' *From Tartan to Tartanry: Scottish Culture, History and Myth*. Ed. Ian Brown. Edinburgh: Edinburgh UP, 2010. 32–47.

Rebellato, Dan. '"And I Will Reach Out My Hand with a Kind of Infinite Slowness and Say the Perfect Thing": The Utopian Theatre of Suspect Culture.' *Contemporary Theatre Review* 13.1 (2003): 61–80.

———. 'Playwriting and Globalisation: Towards a Site-Unspecific Theatre.' *Contemporary Theatre Review* 16.1 (2006): 97–113.

Reid, Trish. 'Anthony Neilson.' *Modern British Playwriting: The 1990s*. Ed. Aleks Sierz. London: Methuen, 2012. 137–63.

———. '"Deformities of the Frame": The Theatre of Anthony Neilson.' *Contemporary Theatre Review* 17.4 (2007): 487–98.

———. '"From Scenes Like These Old Scotia's Grandeur Springs": The New National Theatre of Scotland.' *Contemporary Theatre Review* 17.2 (2007): 192–201.

Riach, Alan. *Representing Scotland in Literature, Popular Culture and Iconography: The Masks of the Modern Nation*. Basingstoke, UK: Palgrave Macmillan, 2005.

Schoene, Berthold, ed. *The Edinburgh Companion to Contemporary Scottish Literature*. Edinburgh: Edinburgh UP, 2007.

Scott, Walter. *Minstrelsy of the Scottish Border: Consisting of Historical and Romantic Ballads, Collected in the Southern Counties of Scotland; With a Few of Modern Date, Founded upon Local Tradition*. Edinburgh: A. Constable, 1802.

Scullion, Adrienne. 'Contemporary Scottish Women Playwrights.' *The Cambridge Companion to Modern British Women Playwrights*. Ed. Elaine Aston and Janelle Reinelt. Cambridge: Cambridge UP, 2000. 94–118.

———. 'Self and Nation: Issues of Identity in Modern Scottish Drama by Women.' *New Theatre Quarterly* 17.4 (2001): 373–90.

Sierz, Aleks. *Decades of Modern British Playwriting: The 1990s*. London: Methuen, 2012.

———. *In-Yer-Face Theatre*. London: Faber & Faber, 2001.

Sierz, Aleks, Martin Middeke, and Peter Schnierer, eds. *The Methuen Drama Guide to Contemporary British Playwrights*. London: Methuen, 2011.

Stevenson, Randall, and Gavin Wallace, eds. *Scottish Theatre since the Seventies*. Edinburgh: Edinburgh UP, 1996.

Tiffany, John. 'Director's Note.' *The National Theatre of Scotland's Black Watch*. By Gregory Burke. London: Faber & Faber, 2007. ix–xii.

Todd, Margo. *The Culture of Protestantism in Early Modern Scotland*. New Haven, CT: Yale UP, 2002.

Wallace, Clare. 'David Harrower.' *The Methuen Drama Guide to Contemporary British Playwrights*. Ed. Aleks Sierz, Martin Middeke, and Peter Schnierer. London: Methuen, 2011. 243–60.

Whyte, Christopher. 'Masculinities in Contemporary Scottish Fiction.' *Forum for Modern Language Studies* 34.3 (1998): 274–85.

index

acknowledgements

Particular thanks go to my editor, Dan Rebellato, for giving this project the go-ahead and for his encouraging and insightful comments. I am equally grateful to Kate Haines and Jenni Burnell at Palgrave Macmillan for their guidance and patience. Like most scholars I am indebted to my colleagues for their constant support. I would especially like to thank Colin Chambers, Ian Brown and Jackie Smart, without whom I would be considerably less sane than I am today. My thanks also go to my partner Andy Lavender. Finally, I am truly honoured that Anthony Neilson has contributed the foreword for this book. His work has been a source of delight to me for many years.